recipes for
fostering

SHARING FOOD AND STORIES **BUILDING RELATIONSHIPS**

DR ANDREA WARMAN

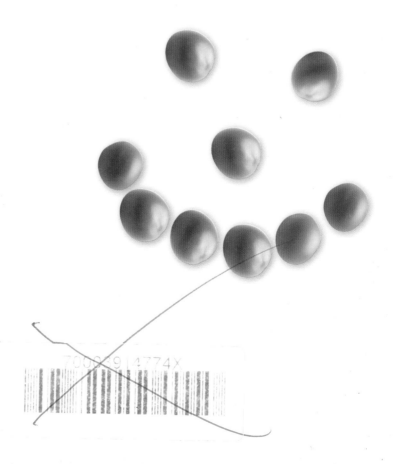

Published by
British Association for Adoption & Fostering
(BAAF)
Saffron House
6-10 Kirby Street
London EC1N 8TS
www.baaf.org.uk

Charity registration 275689 (England and Wales) and SC039337 (Scotland)

British Library Cataloguing in Publication Data
A catalogue record for this book is available from the British Library

ISBN 978 1 905664 63 4

Researcher and Author: Dr Andrea Warman
Home Economist: Katherine Ibbs
Nutritionist: Fiona Hunter
Photography: Sara Jane Haggerty
Design: Owl Graphics Ltd
Printed in Great Britain by The Lavenham Press

BAAF is the leading UK-wide membership organisation for all those concerned
with adoption, fostering and child care issues.

FOREWORD

It gives me great pleasure to introduce *Recipes for Fostering.*

 As we worked on this publication I returned time and again to my own reasons for becoming a foster carer. This means going right back to my childhood when I was never allowed to go out to play with other children. I'd sit on my own, nose pressed up against the window, just watching. If I could, I'd bring home any scruffy urchin I could find – only to be scolded by my mother. So I vowed that when I grew up, I would buy a big house and I would fill it with children's laughter.

These feelings grew stronger when I heard about my uncle who'd been sent to Canada as a child migrant after the death of his parents. It never seemed right to me, and this was confirmed when I found out later on that he'd had a terrible time.

Unfortunately, I continued to be a great disappointment to my mother, failing my eleven plus and then my thirteen plus. I never did get the promised bike. So I left school at fifteen with no qualifications, but was so excited to be offered a job at Lee Castle Hospital looking after children with disabilities. My mother was not happy though, and she found me a different job in a men's outfitters! Not surprisingly, that didn't last long and then I became pregnant – a great scandal in those days.

Even though I was a very young mother, I loved bringing up my four daughters and became involved in a local playgroup. I went on to open my own home nursery, and then spent twenty-five years as a foster carer. So it really was children, children and more children all the way!

Then I heard about Sophie, who had been sexually abused, had been in care since she was six and, aged nine, was in a residential unit because foster carers simply could not cope with her. By then I was a very experienced carer, and I believed that with the right support package I would be able to manage. Sophie's social worker, Jim Cockburn, agreed with me, and after a protracted fight I managed to get the support she needed from her local authority and she came to live with me.

Jim and I were inspired by this and we felt that there were so many other children who could be helped too if only their foster carers were supported and paid adequately. And so we went on to become partners in life and to set up our own fostering agency, Foster Care Associates.

This is my story, and you may ask what has it got to do with this book? Well, I've continued to be fascinated by why and how other people get involved in fostering, and I believe that if we have a better understanding of their backgrounds then we will be able to address the current shortage of foster carers. I think that when you read these stories you too will become fascinated by the motivation to foster. These are ordinary people – but they are doing extraordinary things. I think they are wonderful stories and I hope that they will inspire and encourage others – not just the clever and the well-educated, but people who have overcome adversity and who can understand disadvantage. I hope that some of these people will think about children in need across the world, and consider whether they too could become a foster carer.

Jan Rees,
Non Executive Director, FCA

INTRODUCTION

Recipes for Fostering is the result of a long journey which began as a BAAF development project. We had received funding from the Children's Workforce Development Council to carry out practitioner-led research exploring what it means to be a foster carer. The project focused on two foster carers, and it was their experiences and words with photographs of their everyday lives which formed the basis of the publication, *Who am I and What do I do?* (BAAF, 2007).

During the course of that project, I had spent a good deal of time with the carers, Rosamond and Suzy, and was struck by their practical strategies for welcoming children and young people into their homes. Their awareness of the importance of meal times as well as shopping, cooking and eating together was very clear. Yet there appeared to be very little published research looking at the part food plays in fostering.

I was therefore delighted when Foster Care Associates gave us the opportunity to begin a new project which could focus on this theme. They were keen to use the same research approach, and so I was able to work closely once again with Sara and Karen from Owl Graphics. This time, Katharine, a home economist, and Fiona, a nutritionist, also joined the team.

We chose ten foster care households: three in the Midlands, three from the West of England and four in the London area. They are a mix of local authority and FCA carers, from a wide range of backgrounds and had been involved in many different kinds of fostering.

I began by talking with these carers about how food relates to what they do, and they shared their experiences and their recipes with me. But it very quickly became evident that they all had much bigger stories to tell. Stories about their families, their own histories, their motivation to foster, the children and young people they had looked after – and their feelings about all of these things.

home respect family comfort heritage history acceptance faith memories resourceful

I like to tell stories and I love to listen to them. More importantly, with a background in social anthropology, I can recognise the value of using oral history and life stories as the basis for good research. Foster carers are clearly keen to share their stories, but I am not sure that we have always been ready to hear them, or especially to use what they tell us to improve our understanding of the fostering role.

Listening to these stories confirmed for me that building relationships with the children they look after lies at the heart of what foster carers do. These relationships may be more straightforward as there are carers who go on to adopt the children they foster. Yet, equally significant, are relationships which are made with children and young people who only live in the carer's household for a relatively short time. Or carers who choose for very good reasons to continue being a foster carer, even though they see the children and young people they are bringing up as members of their families. And there are also carers who will always be there for adults whom they fostered as teenagers, becoming grandparent figures for a new generation of children.

The stories presented in this publication do illustrate how, in their own extremely sensitive ways, foster carers use food as part of this process of building and continuing their relationships with children and young people. We hope that all readers will enjoy trying the recipes they have shared with us, that their example will encourage other foster carers to reflect on the meaning of food for the children they are looking after, and that more carers will think about how cooking and eating together creates lasting bonds.

However, I believe that the stories do more than this, and that they also tell us something about the very essence of the fostering role. Making relationships with children in this context is obviously complex, can be messy and the adults who can do it well have very special qualities. Some of these are summed up in the key words which accompany each carer's story. Jackie's **Acceptance** of children with special needs whose backgrounds and futures are very different from her other children; Vernon and Jennifer's recognition of the importance of each child's understanding of their **History**, and the part they have played in it; Dee's ability to draw upon her own, sometimes painful, **Memories** to connect with those she fosters; Sally's great sense of **Family** that is open to new members; Monica's **Respect** for young people with backgrounds different from her own; Sandie's ability to provide **Comfort** for a very troubled young woman; Stella's skills in helping children to feel proud of their **Heritage**; Justin and Dan's **Resourceful** attitude to life which they use to engage and encourage the teenager in their care; Andi's **Home** which provides a safe place for those who have no one else to turn to; and Abid and Shabnam's lasting **Faith** in the children they care for.

We must not forget about the significance of these personal qualities in all of the debates about the future of foster care. So the opportunity to hear the voices of the carers and to read their own words in the pages that follow should be an important reminder to policy-makers and practitioners.

Being involved in this project meant that I was able to make my own relationships with the foster carers presented in *Recipes for Fostering*. So I feel it is important to note that although they come from diverse backgrounds and have very different ways of being, they all share a generosity of spirit, warmth and, above all, a commitment to caring for children who are not their own. I find that deeply moving, uplifting and believe that this particular quality should be far more highly valued. I think that you will agree.

Andrea

Dr Andrea Warman, Fostering Policy, Research and
Development Consultant for the
British Association for Adoption and Fostering (BAAF)

CONTENTS

Jackie and her husband Alan are local authority foster carers in Tamworth who look after children with special needs. Jackie's recipes are **Porridge and Dried Apricots and Fruit Smoothie**

Jackie

acceptance

'In the morning I'm always on the go, getting everyone off on time.'

Taking an interest

'I'd had six children, and they were aged from sixteen down to the youngest who was a year old. And we had our business which I was running, a hairdressers' – I'm a hairdresser and I had my own little shop. Well, opposite the shop was a bus stop and I'd see this lovely young lad, Timothy, he was called, who'd get off the bus and started coming in and making us girls a cup of tea. You see, he was living in a residential home around here, and we found out that he really loved his chocolate. But in the home he'd have to hide it, or another of the kids would eat it. He had special needs, cerebral palsy, and although he was actually about fifteen, it was as if he was about seven or eight, and I think some of the others picked on him a bit. So, it got to the stage where we knew what time the bus was coming, and in he'd come for his bar of chocolate, a little chat, and make us the worst cup of tea I've ever had. His way of saying thanks!'

Jackie became very fond of Timothy and wanted to find out more about his situation.

'When Christmas was coming we asked him, what are you doing for Christmas? And it seemed like all the children in the home bar him were going back to their parents. But he was going to be staying in the home, the only one there. Alan and I talked about it. The idea of him being there without a proper family Christmas really got to me. So, we enquired, and we asked if he could come to us. And in the end we got permission. That was the start. A bond was formed, and he began to come to us regularly for time out from the home. Not permanently, he liked his set routine. But for short holidays and special occasions. For the next three years, he spent those times with us.'

This relationship made Jackie and Alan more aware of children and young people whose parents felt unable to cope, and who needed long-term care.

'Things didn't go well for Timothy when he got to eighteen and he was moved somewhere else. He went downhill. It was all very sad, and it made me so angry. When I talked to my priest about it he said, the only thing I can tell you is, don't get mad, get even. I said, what do you mean, how do I get even? And he said, well, why don't you and Alan foster? Take one child out of the system. I know you could do it. That made us think seriously. And we decided to try. Our eldest, Emma, was about to leave home, giving us more room. But we said from the start that we wanted to look after children with special needs. Because of Timothy. Knowing that there were so many children like him living in homes.'

This is how it is

Jackie and Alan have now been foster carers for their local authority for over eight years.

'From the start we always had long-term placements. That's what we wanted. And always children with disabilities. I say a child with disabilities, not a disabled child, because you learn to adjust and adapt. And then, in time, and without realising it, you don't see that disability any more. The first little girl who came to us was six, but she'd spent her life in a cot. Just curled up in a ball. Never been held or loved. It would be easy to blame her parents. But we've realised over the years that you can't make those judgements. Because they were from a village in the Yemen and when we looked up where she was from on the internet we could see the poverty there. It was unbelievable… And she was severely epileptic. So you could try to understand how it might have been for them. Well, over time – and she was with us for three-and-a-half years – she could sit up, eventually crawl, walk and then go up and down the stairs. From having no facial recognition at all, she was able to tap the table for food, bang her plastic cup for a drink. She even became vocal. She couldn't speak, but you could understand the high pitches and the low pitches, you could talk with her.'

The two brothers who came to live with the family as a toddler and a four-year-old are now eight and eleven.

'Their mum was very young when she had them, and there had been all kinds of problems. They had been living with different relatives and they were very

'From the start we always had long-term placements. That's what we wanted.'

'He'll always need us and the family, even as an adult. So we've set up a trust fund for him, like all our other children.'

unsettled. When we put them down to sleep the first night it was quite clear that they had never slept in a bed. The older boy took a towel from the bathroom – bearing in mind he was only four himself – and he took his baby brother out of the cot, and snuggled down on the towel. And he was going to sleep there in the corner of the bedroom snuggled up on the towel with the baby. I said to Alan, we can't force him into a bed, not now, not in a strange home that they don't even know. So what we did was, we took a quilt and persuaded him to swap the towel for the quilt, kind of rolled them up in the quilt and let them sleep like that, cuddled together.'

Over time the boys settled in.

'The youngest has been with us since he was fourteen months and he's grown up here. He gets extra help at school, but we think he'll do OK. But his brother

'The boys have a brilliant social worker. We've got a great manager of fostering. And we need the system that supports us to keep doing what we do.'

finds things more difficult. He'd spent more time living with a lot of disruption and he still struggles to communicate and socialise. It's got better, but he can still only really cope with one friend at a time. So when it came time to go to senior school we knew he wouldn't manage. He has very serious learning difficulties and finds it very hard to remember things. His social worker was amazing though, and fought to get a statement for him, and he did. It was such a relief. And so he got into a special school where he really likes going.

Even so, we realise that he will always need support. He'll always need us and the family, even as an adult. I see it like a jigsaw puzzle. A child's life can be like that puzzle, with pieces on the side waiting to be put into place. And you as the carer try to put the pieces in, week by week, month by month – until it's complete. But sometimes, there might still be the odd piece missing that you can't put in. You just can't. Because they lost that before they got to you.'

A different kind of family life

Jackie and Alan did think about adopting these boys, but decided to continue being their long-term foster carers for a number of reasons.

'We were prepared to do it, but when we thought it through and discussed it, we were worried about them losing touch with their roots. You see, although they've no contact with their dad, their mum has always been around. And when she was very, very poorly not long ago, we all decided that the boys needed to know. So we carefully explained. Although they didn't want to go and see her in hospital, the older one said he would pray that she'd get better. I've never seen a child so determined. She did get better, and he actually said, that's my prayers that fixed her, wasn't it? And I said yes, you're a wonderful boy. It was so lovely.

So we didn't want to do anything that might break the bond that is there, and we did want them both to still see their nana, who looked after them a lot before they came to us. But above all, we really didn't want to lose the help we get as foster carers. As I said, the boys have a brilliant social worker. We've got a great manager of fostering here. And we are very aware that

we need the system that supports us to keep doing what we do.'

Jackie's household is a very busy one, especially in the mornings.

'Our older children have now moved on. In fact, Emma has three children of her own. But we've still got Edward here who's at college doing a course to be a plumber, and Samuel who got an academic scholarship and is a boarder, though he's here at weekends and holidays. So with the two boys as well, I'm always on the go, getting everyone off on time.'

But she's very keen that they all eat properly before they leave.

'A lot of the children who've been here haven't always had a good diet. And I've always believed that if you feed children well, they will be well. Especially at breakfast. My own nan always said, breakfast like a king. Eat like a prince at lunchtime and a pauper in the evening. Because breakfast is the most important meal of the day. It sets you up. So, in winter, I like to

'In the winter I like to make porridge and add some fruit. And in the summer, you can use natural products to make a smoothie.'

make all the difference, particularly for the children we look after who need to keep healthy.'

Looking to the future

Jackie and Alan may not have adopted the two boys, but they are very much part of the family.

'They're our children. In the event of Alan and I passing away, we've set up a trust fund. They'll be looked after, just like our other children. And because we know they'll always need that support, our daughter Elizabeth went through the full process to become their back-up foster carer. That means that if, for any reason, we couldn't look after them, she would immediately become their guardian. That's something that she really wanted to do.'

People might wonder why, after bringing up their own large family, the couple have taken on this kind of responsibility. Jackie explains.

'My own mum died very young. At forty-nine. The same age I am now. But at her funeral there were twenty-one cars full of people because in that short time she'd impacted on people's lives. She was special. I was so proud to think how much she was thought of, and I'd like to think that when our time comes they might say, what a loss. Life is so precious! And a lot of these kids haven't had an easy life, might never have it easy. But if we can give them something that makes their life better, then we'll give it to them.'

make porridge and add some fruit. Ring the changes to encourage them to eat it up. Apricots are good. But so are other kinds of fruit depending on the season. And there's nothing wrong with using dried fruits as long as you re-hydrate them with a good juice. Then in the summer, if that's a bit heavy, you can make your own muesli. Or use natural products to make a smoothie. Blend up your fruit with natural yoghurt. Add some honey if you want to make it a bit sweeter.

People worry that fresh fruit can be expensive, but if you shop locally you can pick it up quite cheaply – even some of the supermarkets are sourcing the local products now. It doesn't have to cost a lot and it can

Porridge and Dried Apricots

Preparation Time: 5 minutes, plus soaking
Cooking Time: 3-4 minutes
Serves: 1

INGREDIENTS

60g/2oz (10-12) dried apricots, halved, or any dried fruit of your choice
A few drops vanilla extract (optional)
1 x sachet microwave oats
Milk
Honey or sugar, to taste

METHOD

1. The evening before, soak the apricots in just enough water to cover them. Stir in the vanilla extract.
2. The next morning, drain the apricots, then microwave on HIGH for 45 seconds.
3. Make the porridge according to the packet instructions.
4. Serve topped with the apricots and a drizzle of honey or a light sprinkling of sugar.

ALTERNATIVES

Fresh chopped pears soaked in apple juice overnight are a great alternative to apricots. Or try microwaving a chopped apple with 4tbsp of water.

Jackie's Tip:
'Not all children like porridge, but I make it more interesting by adding different toppings.'

Jackie's Tip:
'Use seasonal fruits in your smoothies, and it's less expensive if you shop locally.'

Fruit Smoothie

INGREDIENTS

115g/4oz frozen mixed summer berries
1 x small banana (approx 115g/4oz), peeled and quartered
150ml/5fl oz mango and apple fruit juice

METHOD

1. Mix the juice, berries and banana in a blender until smooth!

FIONA our nutritionist says

Breakfast, as the word suggests, literally means 'breaking the fast'. After 10–12 hours without food our blood sugar is low and our body needs fuel. This is why many nutritionists consider breakfast to be the most important meal of the day. A good healthy breakfast will set you up for the rest of the day. In fact, studies show that what you eat at breakfast can affect your mood, physical and mental performance, weight and your long-term health.

Vernon and Jennifer are short-term local authority foster carers in Plumstead. Their recipe is **Blackberry and Apple Crumble**

Jennifer

Vernon

history

'Their life in care can be so erratic sometimes. So we think it's important to do a life story, something that will go with them.'

14

Short-term foster care

Jennifer didn't work outside the home until their sons started secondary school, when she began a course at her local college with the aim of updating her skills.

'One afternoon a member of the group was saying, I need to leave early because I have to go and collect my child now, my foster child who's been having contact. And I didn't know what contact was, had never known what fostering was. So I asked her, she explained it all, and I thought, well, we have to do a project for this course and I'm going to do fostering for my project. I contacted the borough and they sent me papers about it. But then they followed it up, called me, found out more about us. Said, ooh, you're actually good candidates yourselves for foster care. You're a black couple and we need black carers. So I suppose in a way we just kind of fell into this, it snowballed, just took off.'

The couple went on to be approved and became short-term foster carers for their local authority.

'We fostered for them for about fifteen years, and now another seven with Southwark, and we've probably looked after over a hundred children in that time. People think when you say you are a short-term carer that it's just for a few weeks, but it's not always like that. The little girl who left us a few weeks ago, she was just ten days old when she arrived, and she was three-and-a-half when she left. She'd spent a big part of her life with us.'

This child is going to be adopted, but others will go on to a long-term foster placement or return to live with their birth families. However, as Vernon explains, they all share a need to make sense of what has happened to them.

'Their life in care is so erratic sometimes. Children moving on who don't have a sense of where they are going. We've had children here who've had three, four, even five moves. So Jennifer and I think it's so important to do a life story, something that will go with them. Something that will give them a sense of where they've come from and who they are.'

The couple take photographs, keep a record of events and create a very special book which stays with the child.

'One little girl we had here at three weeks old. She'll be nine in November but she still refers to her life story. Sometimes her mum's phoned up and said, you know, she's a bit worried. She's been looking at her book, and you're fading slightly, can we come and see you? So of course we'll say yes, and they'll come for Sunday lunch and she's, oh, I remember that room. I remember that chair. And it'll all come back to her. The nine-year-old who was three weeks old when she arrived, and we're part of her story.'

Getting the support you need

Inevitably, and despite all their experience, the couple admit it can still be very difficult when children leave.

'Our last little one, she's been gone three weeks now, and we're still sort of grieving.' Vernon describes how this feels for him.

'It's easy to prepare them for adoption, but them actually going is what hurts. Because you worry about what they are doing. Are they eating, sleeping, getting up, in their routine? You worry about everything, even though you know it is for the best and you know the child is going to be happy in their new home. But you just can't help the fact that you sit there and you worry. The other day, I passed the school where I took her every morning and I had a tear in my eye. And in the house I've got to pass her room to go to my bed, and so every night I think, I'll just pop in and see she's OK. But she's not there any more. You know, it's like someone taking something

'I've brought up two children of my own. Looked after over a hundred more now. But each child is different, and as a carer you have to understand.'

'One of the girls we recently fostered has no family here. I'll be writing to her about once a month, until we know she's found her feet.'

away from you that you just don't want to let go of!'

At these times it's very important to get the right kind of support and Vernon values the training that their agency provides.

'It's important to know what resources are out there. I know there are people who you can call upon. And that goes for when I need some strategies too. When I'm at my wits' end, when I need something positive to do, and somewhere to go with this child. In fact, my best training course was about managing difficult behaviour and that really opened my eyes and made me a lot more understanding. It helped me not to take things personally when a child is doing certain things that upset you. Not to get personally caught up in the emotion of the child, and your own reaction, your own emotions, so that it becomes a conflict. Yes, I've brought up two children of my own. Looked after over a hundred more now. But suddenly one can come along that you can't figure out. Each child's attitude and manner is totally different, and as a carer you have to understand. That's how training helps. Teaches you to take a step back, and think about where that particular child is coming from, and how you can respond.'

Jennifer turns to her own mother.

'My mum's my sounding board. When I've had a bad day or I'm upset I'll talk to her. She'll listen and then go, well, why do you do it? I've told you that you don't have to do it. But you know you enjoy it. Now relax for a moment, then go and have a shower. Get ready for tomorrow!'

And both appreciate their relationships with other foster carers.

'We've got long-standing friends from fostering. From when we started doing this. There's about eight of us who went through panel at the same time and they're still like an informal support network. We all sound off, meet up, exchange ideas and just be there for each other. And we've even had holidays together, so our foster children all know one another too. It's like another little family, a little network.'

Making connections

Vernon and Jennifer see their role as preparing children to move on to a more permanent home, but they recognise that they have formed relationships with these children, and they do keep in touch.

'A lot of the ones who've been adopted, we've met their new family and they'll keep sending us photos and school reports over the years.'

Jennifer never forgets a birthday, and sends cards to most of the children they have looked after. She also loves to write letters.

'One of the girls we fostered recently is Vietnamese and has no family here. She starts "uni" later this month so she got a "Congratulations on passing your exams" card and then, "All the best for settling in". And I'll be writing to her about once a month, until we know she's found her feet.'

She recently went to Ireland as a guest at the wedding of the sister of children they fostered many years ago, while Vernon has a very special place in the lives of some of the young men they have cared for.

'We looked after two brothers, and later on one of them got into some trouble, and I went to see him in prison. It meant a lot to him, that visit. Told me, oh, you're the only dad I ever had. He had drifted away, discovered another road to travel, got into trouble. And when he looked back and remembered his time here, he remembered he'd been happy. Anyway, when I saw him there he'd said, oh, as soon as I'm out I'll be visiting you again. Three years passed by and nothing. Then one evening we were sitting here and the door knocked and Jennifer opened it. He

'We listen to each other, come together and then decide - right that's where we're going to go.'

said, hello, and she looked at him and said, I don't know you! He was twenty-three and grown so tall, so big! A big, tall lad now with a girlfriend, learning to drive, working. And since then he phones us up, comes with his brother. We see them both regularly.'

Being flexible

For short-term foster carers, life can be quite unpredictable at times.

'We may get a call from Duty with an emergency placement, we may have to change plans we have

made at short notice. But more than that, you have to have an open mind, because you are going to meet children from all kinds of backgrounds, with all kinds of histories.'

Both agree that having a sense of humour is a very important quality, but so is the ability to be patient and honest.

'We've learned that they are going to test every boundary and that there are no quick fixes. And you can't forget to talk to the kids. Age-appropriate, of course. But they do know why they are here. They

know that their mum has a drink problem or takes drugs. It's no good saying, oh mum will be fine in a few days and you'll go home. Because they know where they're coming from. You know, she fell down the stairs last week, she's not going to get better next week. So if you try to gloss it over, it's going to confuse them more. You'll just lose their trust. Because they've nothing to feel guilty about. It's not their fault that they're in care. Above all, you have to try to find a way to explain to them that it's not a bad thing, they don't have to feel ashamed and that we are there for them.'

Running a flexible household that can respond to different children's needs means thinking carefully about food and mealtimes.

'It can be like Fred's café in here sometimes. You don't like jacket potatoes and you don't like salad, but she does. So she can have jacket potatoes and salad. You prefer macaroni cheese? OK, then that's what you'll have. So it's like, no hard and fast rules.'

The couple share a Caribbean heritage, but they do all kinds of cooking.

'Jennifer can't cook Caribbean!'

'I can cook Caribbean! But basically, I mostly do things like shepherd's pie, spaghetti bolognaise. Spaghetti always goes down well with most children. And some just want the pasta with cheese on top. That's OK, I can respect that. And the good thing about spaghetti is that it stretches, doesn't it? A child may arrive who is hungry, who you hadn't planned for, but you can stretch that bolognaise, can't you?'

Home-made crumble also goes a long way.

'It's a favourite pudding here because you can make a huge dish of it. And if it doesn't all get eaten you can have some the next day too. You can also

'It's like, serve yourself and find a seat. The choice is there, and YOU can put on your plate whatever it is you want to eat.'

'Crumble's a favourite pudding because you can make a huge dish of it. You can also vary the filling depending on the season.'

vary the filling depending on the season – blackberry and apple in the autumn, soft fruit in summer. And it's one where the kids can help out. Making the crumble, stirring the custard. Even picking the fruit the day before.'

Sundays are special because their sons may drop by with their partners and children, and everyone is encouraged to join in.

'The other week we had a really full house! People bring things. My auntie's macaroni cheese. Andrew's mother-in-law is Pakistani and she sent chicken balti. We had three types of rice. And everyone just helped themselves. It was like, serve yourself and find a seat. We always do that here. Not just Sundays, but every day. I don't dish up. Then the choice is there, and you can put on your plate whatever it is *you* want to eat.'

Working together

Vernon and Jennifer are joint carers and this works well for them.

'Vernon loves all sports and he tries to encourage those interests with the children who come to us. He's the one who'll pick them up from youth club, go and watch them play.'

'Yes, I do seem to spend many cold Saturdays in winter on the football field, sort of shivering and drinking tea to keep warm. To the extent that sometimes I do think, another boy! Oh my God, not football again!...But seriously, I know that having a man in their lives does make a difference. We do enjoy each others' company, to the extent that sometimes Jennifer has to say, turn off that football – I want my living room back!'

By sharing the fostering role, they have opportunities to discuss how they might approach particular issues.

'Jennifer and I, we always have different views on certain things, which is good. I think one way, she thinks the other. We might be facing a problem with a child and I'll say, I think we should do so and so. And she'll say, no, no, no. Let's do it like this. But we can listen to each other, come together and then decide – right, that's where we are going to go.'

And most importantly, they can be there for each other.

'Years ago, when I was coming home from work, my great solace was sitting in the car listening to classical music to relax me. Because I'd been so wound up from the day that I just wanted that moment of serenity. And now, I got lucky. Somehow I got Jennifer, and, no matter what is going on here, that's what she gives to me.'

Blackberry and Apple Crumble and Custard

Preparation Time: 25 minutes
Cooking Time: 35-40 minutes
Serves: 6

INGREDIENTS

For the crumble
680g/1½lb cooking apples, peeled, cored and sliced
115g/4oz light brown soft sugar
2 tbsp lemon juice
250g/9oz fresh blackberries, rinsed
85g/3oz unsalted butter, diced
170g/6oz plain flour
85g/3oz caster sugar

For the custard
500ml/18fl oz whole milk
4 medium egg yolks
3 tbsp caster sugar
½ tsp vanilla extract or
1 vanilla pod, split

METHOD

1. Preheat the oven to 200C/400F/ Gas Mark 5.
2. Put the apples, 85g/3oz of brown sugar, lemon juice and 2 tbsp of water in a medium saucepan. Cook gently over a low-medium heat for 5 minutes or until just softened.
3. In a bowl, mix together the black-berries with the remaining brown sugar.
4. Spoon the apples into a 2 pint ovenproof dish then scatter over the blackberries.
5. In a medium-sized mixing bowl, rub the butter into the flour with your fingertips until it looks like fine breadcrumbs. Stir in the caster sugar.
6. Sprinkle the crumble topping mixture evenly over the fruit and press down lightly.
7. Bake for 30 minutes or until crisp and golden.
8. Meanwhile, make the custard. In a medium saucepan, gently bring the milk just to the boil. (If using a vanilla pod, add it here.)
9. In a medium-sized bowl, whisk together the egg yolks and caster sugar until pale. Whisk the hot milk into the egg yolks then pour the egg and milk mixture back into the pan and stir continuously over a low heat until the custard thickens. Stir in the vanilla extract (or remove the vanilla pod).
10. Serve.

FIONA our nutritionist says

A simple way to help children reach their target of at least 5 fruit and veg a day is to incorporate fruit and vegetables into dishes that they enjoy eating. Five-a-day is only part of the fruit and veg message – we should also be eating a variety of different produce. A good way to do this is to think of the colours of the rainbow and try to eat some fruit and veg from each of the colour bands every week.

Jennifer's Tip:
'Why not try making this crumble with other fruits, such as gooseberries, plums or rhubarb. Try to use what is in season.'

Vernon's Tip:
'If the thought of making your own custard really scares you, the packet variety which has been around for years would never be grumbled at!'

Dee is an FCA foster carer who lives in the Midlands. Her recipe is **Paratha**

Dee

Memories

'It was just us children and our mother who flew out that day. To start a new life in England.'

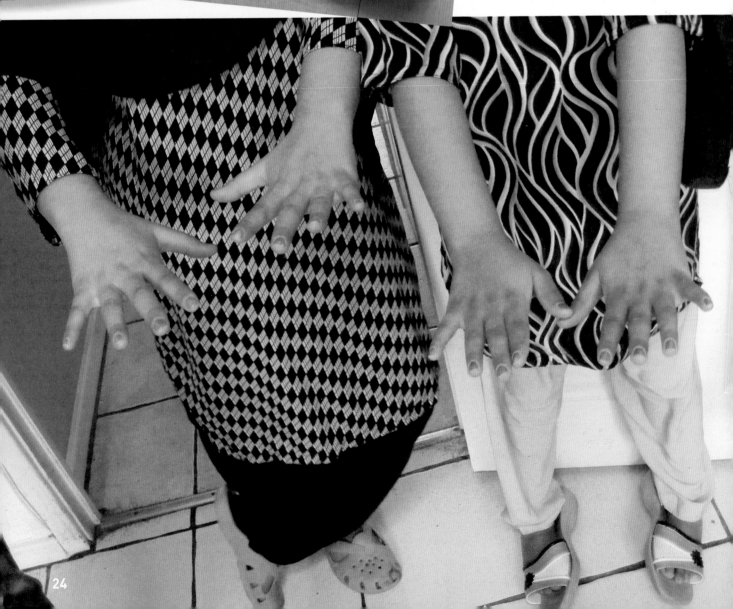

Becoming a refugee

Dee was born in Kenya, but grew up in Uganda where her father had a haulage business. She describes a privileged and idyllic early life, which changed dramatically when she was twelve years old.

'It was just another day at school and we were playing rounders when one of the nuns came and said we must all go home immediately. We had no idea what was wrong. I remember feeling a bit annoyed because my turn to bat was coming. Our driver would usually pick us up, but he just didn't come, and so I started to walk. But on the way we realised something terrible was going on. I was with this boy, Babu. We decided to hide together under some stairs in a building. We had to stay hidden like that all night. And while we were there we saw the soldiers, chasing people, hitting them. Using their machetes. But there was nothing we could do. At about five o'clock in the morning when it was getting light, we ran out. There were people lying bleeding all around. But what could we do? We just ran home as fast as we could. And my parents were so relieved that I was safe. Then my father told us we had to leave immediately. We would be going to England.'

Dee's family, along with others of Asian heritage, were no longer welcome in Uganda, and their father made hasty arrangements to get them to safety. But first there would be another, very frightening journey.

'We had to get to the capital to fly out. About thirty miles from our home. My father had taken others there before us and he had seen what happened to the women. He knew that the soldiers were raping the women and he was frightened for us. So what he did was build this kind of box. My mother and my brother sat in the car. But me and my two sisters were hidden in the box. Where we would be safe. We couldn't eat or drink anything before we left. Just mint to chew. Because although it wasn't very far, it took many hours to get to the airport. Every few minutes we would be stopped and the soldiers would ask questions. Look inside. They never found us.

My father was so happy when we reached our destination. And he cried. I can still see him thanking God that we were safe and kissing us goodbye. Because that was the last we saw of him for a long time. He didn't have a British passport and he had to stay behind. So it was just us children and our mother who flew out that day. To a new life.'

It was very different for the family when they made their home in the Midlands.

'My step-mum stuck by me and helped me in any way she could. She accepted the way I lived my life.'

'My poor mother was suddenly without her husband and had all of us children to look after. Although people were kind to us and we were given a house and warm clothes, it was all still very strange. We wanted to eat what we'd eaten before. Curry, rice, patties. But all we lived on was soup and bread because where we lived there was no Asian shop, and so she couldn't buy anything she needed to cook. But the WRVS women were trying very hard to trace my dad. They were really helping us. And we were going to school, learning English. I was teaching my mum too. Then my brother got a job, driving. I reached sixteen and began nursing training. Over time we began to settle.'

Breaking all the rules

Dee's father was eventually reunited with his family, and despite her happiness at being with him, her life had to change once more.

'I'd been living in the hospital in the nurses' home during the week. Coming back on Friday evenings on the bus. Then on Sunday evenings getting the bus again to the hospital. But he didn't like me staying away like that. He was in no way pleased with that. So I had to give it up. I realised that he was scared for me. He was being protective. But still, it did make me sad because I loved nursing. I ended up working in a factory, which didn't please me. Anyway, over time, I managed to persuade my dad. Because he knew the haulage business and was familiar with it he did agree to let me do my Heavy Goods Vehicle test. And he let me get a job as a lorry driver.'

So, very unusually in the seventies, Dee drove a lorry around the Midlands. Her personal life was also unconventional.

'My family was Hindu and I had an arranged marriage to please my father. But it didn't work out. I later met a Muslim man, converted to Islam, and had my sons with him. After some years I married again, and although that didn't go well, my second husband was like a father to my children and he supported us. I did live on my own though, and I brought up the boys myself. Many people did not approve of what I was doing. My mother had died by this time and my father had a new wife. And it was her, my step-mum, who stuck by me, stayed close to me and helped any way she could. She accepted the way I lived my life. I love her dearly for that, and always will'.

As a lone mother, and with her sons becoming more independent, Dee made another big decision.

'I love children and I felt that I had more to give. I wasn't in a relationship at the time, but I was doing a very good job with my sons. The local council was looking for people from our community who could adopt children. I decided to find out more, and I did all of the training. Some time later I was introduced to the girls, who are sisters. Eventually they came to live with me. They were aged just three and five. And now they are big girls – nine and twelve! My daughters.'

Helping others

Adopting the girls made Dee aware that other children and young people needed a family. She became interested in fostering.

'I'd always talked about how I grew up and what that was like. My eldest boy would often ask, mum how were you with your brothers and sisters? And I'd tell him about how there were seven of us, that we would eat together and that my cousins would sometimes live with us too. A very big family. We had plenty of room in the house in Uganda, you see. And I told the children that my cousins were like my brothers and sisters too. We didn't make any distinctions. I told them how I loved being part of all that. And they said, it would be good if we had more brothers and sisters here. If we could open our home to more children. So I looked around, and I called FCA. And they were so welcoming. They told me that there were many children of Asian heritage in care. So, with my children's permission, I decided to become a foster carer.'

'I grew up as part of a big family, so I wanted to open up our home here to more children. To become a foster carer.'

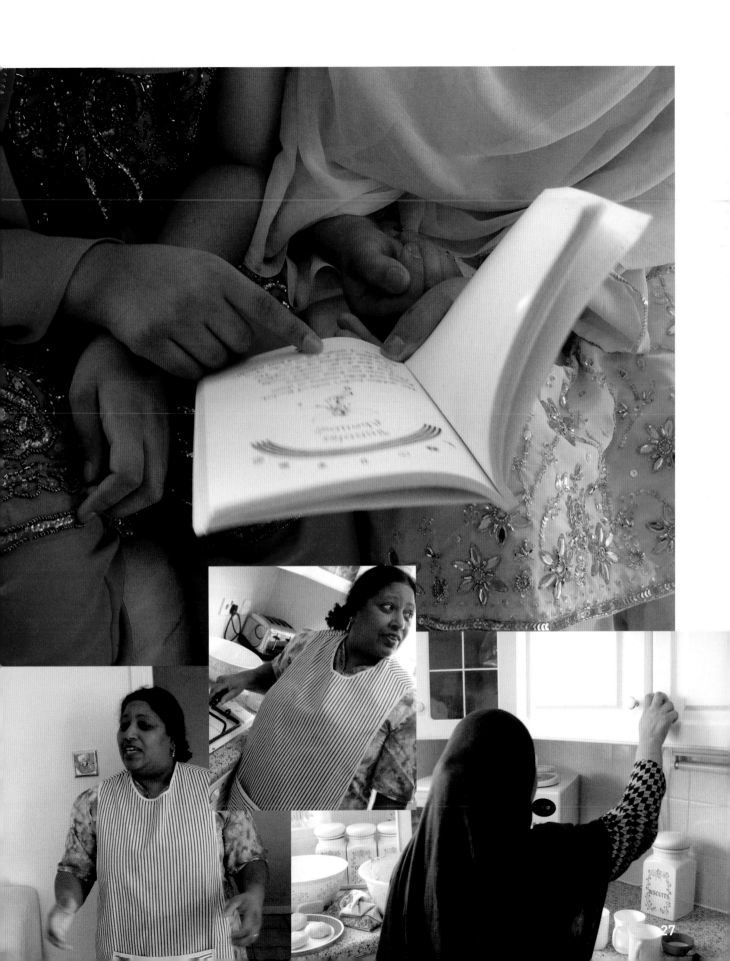

'At the beginning he was quiet,
so I tried to make him feel at home.
To make food that I hoped he would like.'

Dee's own life history helps her to understand the children she now fosters.

'My most recent placement came here to me aged thirteen. He's a refugee. From Afghanistan. Came all the way by lorry. And I knew that he must have had a bad time on that journey. He had to have suffered badly. But at the beginning, he was very, very quiet. Because he didn't know who to trust. Who not to trust. So I tried to make him feel at home. To cook food I hoped he would like.

Then, one morning I decided to make paratha. He was in the bathroom getting ready. Smelled the cooking and joined me in the kitchen. Said, the smell, the smell of the paratha cooking. My mum used to cook that in the morning for me. And I asked, would you like some? He said, oh yes. So I cooked him a paratha, and he stood watching me do it and told me, that smell reminds me of my mum. And you could see the tears in his eyes. I felt really sad for him. So I gave him the paratha and a tea, and I said, well, let's talk about what you remember. Tell me what your mum used to do. Then, he began to talk. He did tell me about his mum and his life at home. And he did tell me about all the things that had happened on his journey.

All of the secrets he'd been keeping inside.'

She also doesn't forget what it means to be far from home and to worry about people you love, but had to leave behind.

'He's been here three years now and he's in school, speaks fluent English as well as Urdu. He's doing really well. Got an award for his business studies and most improved English. But I know how he thinks about his family. So we write to the Red Cross to try to find his mother. His father and his brother aren't there, but his mother – is she alive or….? I know how that is. What he is going through.'

Dee's life has been eventful, sometimes far from easy. Yet now, settled and pleased with how things have worked out for herself and her family, she welcomes the opportunity to give something back.

'I don't forget, but I don't dwell on the past. Always look forward. There's a life in front of us, so learn from your experiences, good and bad, and move on. Fostering makes it possible to give a child a chance, to give them a future. You will learn a lot from it. You will learn from them as much as they will learn from you. And they will keep you going, ready to face whatever is coming next.'

'He smelled the paratha cooking
and said that it reminded him of
his mum. Then, he began to talk.'

Dee's Paratha

Preparation Time: 25–30 minutes
Cooking Time: 20 minutes
Makes: 4 as an accompaniment

INGREDIENTS

170g/6oz plain or wholemeal flour,
plus extra for rolling
A pinch of salt
2 tsp vegetable oil
Approx 100ml/3½fl oz warm water
85g/3oz butter, melted, plus
softened for spreading

METHOD

1. Tip the flour and salt into a
medium sized bowl. Make a well in
the flour, pour in the oil and water
and mix to form a soft dough.
Knead the dough for 10 minutes or
until smooth.
2. Divide the dough into 4 equal
portions. On a lightly floured work
surface, roll out each piece into a
round of 12.5cm/5"-15cm/6" in
diameter.
3. Spread a round of dough with
melted butter, fold it in half, spread
again with butter, and fold it in half
again to form a triangle.
4. Repeat with the remaining 3
portions of dough.

5. Gently roll each buttered
dough into a 15cm/6" – 20cm/8"
round, depending on the final
texture you prefer, ensuring the
middle is no thicker than the
outside edge.
You still want to be able to see
the layers.
6. Place a large sized frying pan
or flat griddle over a medium-
high heat. Put one paratha into
the pan, spread with a knob of
softened butter and fry until
bubbles start to appear on the
surface and brown spots on the
underside. With tongs, turn the
paratha over and again spread
with butter. Cook further until
bubbles and brown spots appear
again.
7. Repeat step 6 until the paratha
is fully cooked through, has
golden marks and is a little crisp.
8. Keep each paratha warm on
a plate covered with foil or in a
sealed tin whilst you cook the
others.

FIONA our nutritionist says

Making bread is some-
thing that children of all
ages enjoy. Getting
children involved in the kitchen
is a great way to educate them
about food and nutrition and
teach them an important life
skill. To boost the fibre content of
breads and cakes, use wholemeal
flour or a 50/50 mix of wholemeal and white.

Dee's Tip:
'Parathas are a great
accompaniment to curries, but
I also like to serve them on their
own with a cup of tea for a
simple breakfast.'

Dee's Tip:
"I like to make my paratha soft yet crispy. For
this, you need to make soft dough, not dough that is
too stiff or sticky. Also, make sure you roll it out
until it is very thin. Practice makes perfect!"

Mom's DINER
Open 24 hours

Sally was born and grew up in South East London. Her recipe is a **Roast Lamb "Roastie" Lunch**

Sally

family

Being part of a big family

Sally was born and grew up in South East London, not far from New Cross where she has settled and continues to live.

'There's eight of us siblings – two boys, six girls, all extremely close. All brought up to kind of look out for one another and, you know…the older ones look after the younger ones and so on, which is something that's been passed down, I guess, through the family. And we all kind of do that now, share things, socialise together – still extremely close.'

Although she describes a very happy childhood, it was not always easy. There was never very much money around, but when her father died things got even tougher.

'My mum's a strong person. Nothing really fazes her, nothing worried her – something always turned up. We lost our dad when I was thirteen, and she managed brilliantly. It's only as you get older that you realise just how much she did do, and how much it must have cost her to do it so well. She stayed on her own, she never had any partner, so her life went on being the home and the children – just her family.'

Sally has great love and respect for her mum.

'Even to this day, my mum is still the person that if any of us have a problem – even though she hasn't been well herself – if we have a problem, or if we need anything or we don't know what to do about some-thing, we go and ask mum what she thinks. Anything. She's always been the one you could talk to. So in your own family you try to do the same. To be kind of available, if you like, especially for your children – just as your mum was for you. Always there. Always available.'

So Sally has aspired to be like her mum, and as she grew up she helped her as much as she could, especially with the care of younger brothers and sisters.

'With my mum being on her own we did all have to muck in. I think I was a dab hand at changing a terry nappy by the time I was about ten. Then between the ages of 40 and 50 she had a lot of illness, even major operations. And I was the one who had to look after the children. There were probably four or five of them that actually still needed looking after. As well as cleaning the home, doing the washing, doing the ironing, doing everything that needed doing. I was just eighteen at the time, and I had John, my own son, to look after as well.'

Not surprisingly, Sally became seen as a "coper" herself.

'I kind of took over that mum role, sort of thing, to everybody in the family. And it's just stuck I think.'

Yet this didn't stop Sally having ambitions, even though she had missed out on her secondary schooling.

'We had moved home when I was around fourteen and we all had to get into new schools. But I was the last one – there was just no place for me. I got lost in the system. They just didn't seem too bothered. And I had loved school, and I missed going, and I missed taking my exams. But then later on, when John was still a baby, I started going to college. I found things I was interested in and started a couple of days a week. I got a real passion for it and did accountancy, then languages. Anything that would sort of propel me if you like, that would serve me well, I did.'

Sally went on to have a career as well as bringing up John and his sister Jo who are now in their late twenties.

'My last position was in a bank, a German investment bank in the City, and yes I did feel proud – thinking about where I'd come from. But I couldn't have done it all without help from the family. Sometimes I'd have to start working at eight o'clock, so one of my sisters would take the children to school, or pick them up, that sort of thing. It worked really well for us.'

Then Sally's children got older, left home and she sadly lost her husband. She found herself in her early forties feeling that her life was good, but that something was missing.

'I remember watching this little girl who lived a few streets away. She was the eldest of five – their mum was on her own and finding it hard I think. She was

'Growing up in a big family was not all rosy as I've said, but the sharing, the closeness, being fair, it's stayed with me. Being fair was a big thing when I was a child. My dad taught me that.'

'I'll always remember the day they arrived. They came up the front steps and introduced themselves. I'd opened a box of chocolates for them, and while I was speaking to the social worker in the kitchen they'd finished the whole box!'

only about six herself but she always seemed to be doing something. This time, I saw her coming back from the corner shop dragging this heavy bag of potatoes. And of course, where it was so heavy and she had to drag it, one by one she was losing the potatoes. So I guess by the time she got home there were probably no potatoes left and she probably got shouted at, even smacked. I looked at her struggling and it took me back to when I was a child – because we didn't have very much but we did have a happy, stable kind of life. I do remember when I had holes in my shoes and had to go to school with a bit of a cornflakes box in the hole so it wouldn't rub on my foot. So it wasn't all rosy, but I do have so many fond, warm memories of that time. And coming back to the little girl, I had a strong feeling that I wanted to help, to get involved.'

Sally talked this over with her friends and one of them suggested contacting her local social services. She did get in touch, and she heard about fostering.

Becoming a foster carer

'I really didn't know what foster carers do, but they talked me through it. Telling me that it was really what I'd been thinking about – looking after children. Giving them that love and care and nurturing and all of the stuff children need. Preparing them to go back to their families, moving them on to new families or even keeping them with you until they're ready to leave home. And I got really excited about it. The more I found out and went into the ins and outs of it all, the

more I thought, yeah, this is what I want to do.'

So she began the process of becoming a foster carer, and shortly after approval Rachel and Craig, five-year old twins, became her first placement.

'I'll always remember the day they arrived. They came up the front steps and introduced themselves. I'd opened a box of chocolates for them, and while I was speaking to the social worker in the kitchen they'd finished the whole box! And everything from that first day we all remember. It was very special. As time went on I really got to know them, their likes and dislikes and of course their difficulties and how to manage those things.'

The twins settled in very well and the staff at their school immediately noticed.

'The school actually pointed out the changes in them. And I got very involved with the teachers and they just kept reporting back on the positives. They were saying, whatever it is that you're doing, you're doing something really good. The children are mixing now, enjoying it all now. I didn't feel that I was doing anything special, just the normal things you do as a family – that I'd done with my family.'

Over time, the twins became very much part of Sally's life.

'I think it was probably about eight or nine months after the children had been with me and obviously I'd been kept informed about what was happening and all the procedures. And my daughter was sitting with me one evening, and we were talking about what would happen if – if and when – the children moved on. And

'We still get together over a meal. Me, my sisters, my nieces and nephews. My granddaughter. When I cook, my son and daughter come down. In actual fact, they'll phone me up and say, are you cooking tonight mum?'

I guess by that time I knew that social services were looking for a permanent family for them. It had never crossed my mind that I would adopt any children myself. But my daughter said, mum I think you need to talk to the social worker about adoption because actually, I don't think you can let the twins go. And it made me really think – I had been quite prepared for them to have a new family, but now, feeling we had come such a long way together – it didn't feel right. So we all had a really big conversation. With my son and my daughter, my granddaughter who was eleven at the time and very close to me. And the rest of the family too. They all gave good feedback – wanted me to do it. They knew I'd just grown to love the twins, and you know they had just slotted in here like the missing piece of a jigsaw. It's like they've always been here.'

Now aged eight, Craig and Rachel have been adopted by Sally and are part of her family.

'I'm a great believer in things that are meant to be, and it all just clicked into place. It just feels right.'

Sharing recipes and food

Sally had been aware that helping the twins to feel comfortable and at home, especially in the early days, was such an important part of the foster carer's role. And in Sally's family, mealtimes have always been a special time.

'Well. Food is a big, big thing for us. Because growing up, we were lots of people coming to the table a couple of times a day, where we'd talk about the day's events and what had gone on. So meals have always been a social event within our family.'

In such a busy household with eight siblings, Sally recognised the value of this rare opportunity to talk things through. Mealtimes were also a time when she could help her mum.

'We was always helping out, you know. Laying the table, dishing the food, later on even doing some of the cooking.'

In fact, Sally says that she learned to cook by watching her mum and still prepares many of the same dishes.

'My dumplings are still bad and I'll phone up and say, mum, how do you do dumplings? Only two weeks ago she talked me through the dumpling procedure yet again! I do my mum's "red stew" which uses tinned tomatoes, and I always do my roasts like she does.'

Craig and Rachel have been introduced to this part of Sally's family life.

'We still get together over a meal. Me, my sisters, my nieces and nephews. My granddaughter. When I cook, my son and daughter come down. In actual fact they'll phone me up and say, are you cooking tonight mum?!'

Although the twins had a different experience of meal times, they now love this family tradition.

'My son and daughter will say, mum let's have a "roastie", even during the week. That's what we call a roast dinner. And the little ones use it as well now. They'll ask for a "roastie" too.'

The twins are very keen to try new things, but a roast dinner has become their favourite too.

'So I'll go, what shall we have for dinner and they'll say, oh mum, let's have a "roastie". And I'll go, not a "roastie" again tonight! And we'll all have a laugh.'

Family life

Family is so important for Sally, but many people might wonder why, at this stage in her life, she has adopted two young children and continues to be a foster carer.

'It's what I get back from them. What I get back from children. How they love me, and how they trust me, and how they change. It's just so rewarding. I'm not saying that it's all positive, because it is hard work But the rewards at the end of it far outweigh the difficult times or, you know, the complex issues that you come across. I sometimes sit here and think, who, me?

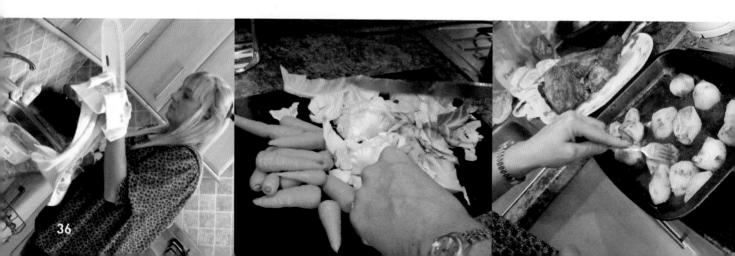

'So I'll go, what shall we have for dinner and they'll say, oh mum, let's have a "Roastie". And I'll go, not a "Roastie" again tonight! And we'll all have a laugh.'

'Well. Food is a big, big thing for us. Because growing up, we were lots of people coming to the table a couple of times a day, where we'd talk about the day's events and what had gone on. So meals have always been a social event within our family.'

I mean, I'm nobody special. I'm special to my family, but…you know, why should I make a difference to anyone else? And yet, I've seen that I have. And that just makes me feel really good.'

And she is very aware that her own experiences have shaped who she is now, and why she does what she does.

'Growing up in a big family was not all rosy as I've said, but the sharing, the closeness, being fair – it's stayed with me. Being fair was a big thing when I was a child…my dad taught me that.'

In fact, she has a strong memory of how he did this.

'I was about five or six and my nan used to have us down to Hastings to her caravan in turns. We'd all take it in turns to go down there with her for the weekend. She was very much into her first grandchild and I did know she favoured my older sister Lorraine – just felt it. But then one time she went down on her own without any of us kids, and when she came back she had this big bag full of sticks of rock – and the most beautiful walky-talky doll. And at that time it was such a big thing – a walky-talky doll – when my nan walked in with it I just fell in love with that doll! She sat down, and I had my eyes on that doll, and Lorraine was looking at it too. And then nan said, there you are, Lorraine, and she gave the doll to my sister who was over the moon. And I felt, where's mine? Where's my doll? And then she put her hands in her bag, and pulled out a stick of rock, said, here's one for you, one for Brian – gave me and the others a stick of rock each. And I just felt so unhappy…Well, my dad must have seen my face, and as my nan got up to go he picked up the doll, took back the rocks, and thrust them into my nan's arms. He said, thanks very much, but take the rocks, take your doll, and until you can treat them all the same Lorraine's not having the doll…What a triumph! Because I thought, yes! My dad was not going to have me treated any different from my sister.'

Sally feels that this incident and her dad's response was a powerful influence over the way she brought up her children.

'It stayed with me. With my children it was the one big thing actually – fairness. How fantastic for Lorraine who was going to be so proud of that walky-talky doll. But how sad was I, because she had one and I didn't. How awful was that? And so, bringing up my children, we've had good times and we've had bad, but if one had something, the other would get it too – I never wanted one to feel left out.'

Now, looking after Rachel and Craig, Sally feels very different from the "young mum" she was, and says that she has learned from some of the mistakes she made with John and Jo.

'But the basic things I do just the same. We're very family-orientated – that stems from the big family that I have, and my experiences of growing up in it. And with Rachel and Craig they are – being twins – they are very sharing and warm with each other. They look out for each other, because I think they only had each other previously. So yeah, they're very warm with each other, and they look out for each other – and I guess that's how I am, and how we do things – and really just a lot like our family have always been.'

Sally's Roast Lamb "Roastie" Lunch

Preparation Time: 10 minutes, plus the vegetables and gravy can be prepared during the first 45 minutes of the lamb cooking.

Cooking Time: approx 2 hours, plus resting, depending on the weight of the lamb and how well cooked you like it. This is based on "medium".

Lamb cooking guide:

20 minutes/lb, plus 20 minutes for rare

25 minutes/lb, plus 25 minutes for medium

30 minutes/lb, plus 30minutes for well done

Serves: 6

INGREDIENTS

For the lamb

1 x 1.825kg–2.270kg/4–5lb leg of lamb

Salt and freshly ground black pepper

4 tbsp oil

For the Yorkshire puddings

145g/5oz plain flour

A pinch of salt

3 medium eggs

300ml/11fl oz full-fat milk

4 tbsp vegetable oil

For the vegetables

1.375–1.825kg/3–4lb King Edward potatoes, peeled and halved (cut into thirds if large)

1 medium (900g/1lb 15¾oz) swede, peeled and chopped

4 large carrots, peeled and sliced

500g/1lb 1½oz greens, washed and shredded

255g/9oz petit pois

60g/2oz unsalted butter

Salt and freshly ground black pepper

Sally's Tip:

'If you prefer, packet gravy and Yorkshire puddings do the trick just as well.'

For the gravy

60g/2oz butter

2 onions, peeled and thinly sliced

30g/1oz plain flour

800ml/28fl oz beef stock

Fat-free juice from cooked lamb

Mint sauce, for serving

METHOD

1. Preheat the oven to 190C/375F/Gas Mark 5.

2. Firstly, prepare the Yorkshire pudding batter. In a medium bowl, sift together the flour and salt. Make a well in the flour then whisk in the eggs and a little of the milk to form a paste. Gradually whisk in the remaining milk until you have a smooth batter. Cover and set aside.

3. Place the lamb in a large roasting tin. Season with salt and pepper then drizzle over the oil. Roast according to your cooking preference. (Meanwhile, prepare your vegetables and gravy.)

4. After 40–45 minutes, baste the lamb and bring the potatoes to boil in a large saucepan of salted water for 5 minutes. Drain the potatoes, shaking well to roughen the edges. Add the par-boiled potatoes to the roasting tin with the lamb, coating them well in the fat. Roast for 30–35 minutes then baste the lamb again and turn the potatoes.

5. After a further 20–25 minutes, bring the swede and carrot to boil in a large saucepan for 25 minutes.

6. After 10–15 minutes, equally divide the oil for the Yorkshire puddings between a 12-hole muffin tin. Place in the oven and heat for 3–4 minutes.

7. Remove the lamb from the oven, cover with foil and leave to rest. Transfer the roast potatoes onto a clean tray and place them back in the oven. (This will allow you to use the lamb juices to make the gravy. Make sure you spoon off the fat first).

8. Carefully take the muffin tin out of the oven and pour equal amounts of the batter into each muffin hole. (I found a ¼ cup measure was really useful to do this.) Bake the Yorkshire puddings for 30–35 minutes or until risen, golden and cooked through.

9. Meanwhile, make the gravy. In a medium saucepan, melt the butter. Add the onion and cook over a medium heat for 4–5 minutes or until softened. Stir in the flour for 1 minute. Pour in the stock and fat-free lamb juice, bring to the boil then simmer for 10–15 minutes or until thickened to your liking. Season.

10. Steam the greens for 10–12 minutes, then season and dot with 15g/½oz butter to serve.

11. Meanwhile, carve the lamb.

12. In a small saucepan, cover the peas in boiled water. Bring back to boil for 2 minutes, then drain and toss in 15g/½oz butter and season.

13. Finally, drain and mash the swede and carrot with 30g/1oz butter then season.

14. Serve.

FIONA our nutritionist says

Family meals provide much more than the opportunity to fill hungry tummies – they provide the chance for families to talk and share feelings. Research shows that children who regularly eat with their families are more likely to eat a healthier diet. Family meals don't need to be elaborate affairs – remember, simple foods served with love and laughter will outshine a gourmet offering any time.

Monica brought up four sons in inner-city Bristol before becoming a carer for FCA three years ago. Her recipe is **Rice and Peas with Pan Fried Fish**

Monica

respect

'We both love cricket! And I'm so pleased that we can get him all the equipment he needs to take part.'

'Going it alone from an early age made me strong and independent. But I wanted my kids to have that love and that foundation until THEY were ready to leave.'

BRISTOL SWEET MART

Doing it on my own

Monica lives in the Easton area of Bristol with her youngest son, who is now in his twenties. She brought up all four of her boys in this part of the inner-city which has been her home for over thirty years.

'Their dad has always been around, but the day-to-day bringing up I did myself. When they got older and they started going into town, certain things started happening to them, and I had to set up rules or routines so that I knew they'd be safe. They always had to ring me. And if they didn't ring me, I'd be on the phone and I'd be ringing around. Because if they didn't call, then I would always worry that something bad could have happened to them.'

When her sons were in their teens one was arrested for a crime he had not committed, another was robbed and had his car stolen, while her son Andre was the victim of a vicious assault.

'He was on a night out with some friends. I think it was the end of the night and there were just two of them together going home. And four boys, big boys, started saying things to him, insulting him. And he was with his friend who happened to be white. Because he always had lots of friends, mixed with lots of friends. And he tried not to take any notice, he was shocked really at what they were doing. But they beat him up so badly, so badly. His friend and his girlfriend took him to hospital, his face all battered and bruised…I can still see it. I was just shock, shock…But we coped. And those things gave me a little bit of strength rather than going under.'

In fact, Monica is very proud of what her sons went on to achieve. They all continued their studies, have successful careers and Andre now works as a professional actor in London.

Looking after young men

Monica was able to draw upon these difficult experiences and the strategies she had used to cope as a lone mother when she began fostering three years ago.

'I was doing support work with adults with learning difficulties living in their own home. Encouraging them to do things for themselves, do their own washing, keeping their house clean. You're just there to give them some guidance. Well, I found I liked doing that. Then my step-sister at the time was doing fostering. She would talk about it, and by then I only had my youngest son still here with me. So I decided that I would give it a go. That I would like to try to give a young person having some troubles a home, and try to see what I could do, and work with it.'

Monica grew up in the Caribbean, but the two young men currently placed with her are from very different backgrounds.

'The first one came to me about eighteen months ago and he's seventeen now. He's white, from a small town round here, but he wanted to live with a black family. So he's a white young man, living in a black household and I'd talked to my own boys about that. They've supported me in all of this. For me, I just believe that a child is a child, and if you're going to give them something, it's the same thing you're going to give. You know, the support and the love. And to be honest, I haven't noticed a lot of difference, haven't felt a lot of difference looking after him. He's got an interest in music and when my sons come here they'll all have a conversation, talk about whatever's on the TV, whatever games, discuss things they all like to do.'

The second was potentially more challenging.

'He's a young Afghani man, a refugee, and he came here in an emergency. And he was a bit unsettled when he came, had been with two other carers before me. But gradually, and gradually he's found his place and he wants to stay. I must say that at the start I didn't know if I would manage because of the language. With the first, there are differences, but we could both speak English and so I knew whatever I would say, he would understand, we could understand each other. But with the second I was more worried that he would be comfortable here, and that it be would be OK for us.'

'People have asked me, aren't you scared? A woman on your own with grown up boys in the house? But they have respected my rules and boundaries from the start.'

'I started buying figs and dates for him from the Asian shops around here.'

Yet Monica was surprised to find that she had more in common with this young man than she expected.

'Yes, we both love cricket! I knew he was very into a lot of sports so I kept supporting him, whatever he wanted to do, I tried to find a way to get him, you know, started. First it was boxing, he did that for a while. And at school, rugby and tennis. But then, the cricket season started, and I realised he was interested, and so he started with the local YMCA team. I watched and watched and I could soon see that this was something he was really committed to. But he was having to borrow from other players, there were things he needed. Then he played one match and he was so brilliant they put his picture in the paper! His social worker was chuffed. We were all proud. And now I'm pleased because they've agreed that we can get him the things he needs, all the equipment he needs to take part.'

So Monica has found ways to communicate with these two very different young men, and their respect for her is also clear.

'People have asked me, aren't you scared? A woman on your own with these grown-up boys in the house with you? But you know, with both, I've had rules and boundaries from the start. About things like what time they need to come in. And if you do need to stay out longer then you need to phone – just like with my own boys. And it's been good, they both do it. With the second, of course, it was harder. I had to start out watching out for him all the time. Because of the language, and he just didn't know how it is here. He was beaten up. On the way home from school. And that was hard, having to cope with that. Especially after what happened with Andre…But he's got on so well with his English, and he's listened and he understands much more now. And he'll say, don't worry Monica, I'm alright, I'm alright…His behaviour has just been so good. He never shouts. He's never been rude to me. He's brilliant.'

Mixing it up

Monica's approach to cooking for her new family has been particularly creative.

'Even my boys were different. Only one of my sons went for his proper Caribbean food. That's my eldest, and he always liked his curry and his rice and peas. So I always did a variety when they were growing up. And now, my fostered boys. One does not like anything spicy. So, say if I was doing chicken, I would put all-purpose seasoning over all the chicken, then take out the piece I was cooking for him and put it on the side. To the rest I would add more seasoning, my paprika, black pepper and curry spice. But leave that off what I cook for him, because I know he doesn't like it, and I don't want to upset his stomach.'

She has recognised the importance of understanding the dietary needs of the young Afghani man, but has also enjoyed learning more about his culture.

'I know he doesn't eat pork, so I never cook that for him. And when he was fasting, he explained to me that he needed something sweet to break the fast. So I started buying figs or dates for that, and going to one of

SQUID RINGS
BATTERED SQUID
BREADED CRAB CLAW
LANGOUSTINE
OYSTER MEAT
PLAICE GOUJONS
FILO PASTRY BRD
BUTTERFLY PRA
FANTAIL CKD &
RAW SHELL O
RAW PEELED

HOT PEPPERS
£8.71 KG

45

the Asian shops around here to buy those things. And for chicken and mutton dishes I buy the halal meat. And I'll eat it, cook with it for everyone. Because I've learned that it's only the way that the animal is killed that is different. The meat tastes the same – better sometimes. You just clean it up, season it up. All in the same way and put it on. So now I go to the halal butcher for most of my meat shopping, to the extent that my old butcher isn't talking to me any more because he's lost a customer!'

And she sometimes adapts traditional Jamaican dishes.

'I'll do a chicken or mutton curry but use halal meat. And if someone doesn't like curry, they'll have rice and peas but with a piece of fish. It might be a piece of battered fish from the fish shop. Or it might be something like red snapper. That works well with the spices and rice. And they all like my fish and the way I cook it.'

Finding your way

Monica has a deep understanding of how important it is to feel comfortable and at home.

'You see, I was brought up in Jamaica by my grandmother. My mother came to this country and she had to leave me there. And my dad didn't really help her. But when she got herself together, she met someone else, they got married and she sent for me. So I came to England when I was twelve. I knew that this lady was here, had always been sending me these clothes and things from England. I had a picture of her to say this was my mum. But my mum in my eyes was my grandmother, the one who'd looked after me all that time. I loved her as my mum, you know. So when I heard I had to leave her it was terrible. I cried and cried. I didn't know what I was coming to. Meeting this strange lady at the airport. It was really hard. Everything was so hard at first. I was homesick, homesick…And the bond with my mother was not there. I just missed my grandmother and I'd write to her and say, I'm coming home. When I'm fourteen, I'm coming home…Just longing for everything I'd left behind.'

She made her own way in this new world from an early age, and had to grow up very quickly.

'It did make me strong and it's made me independent. But I didn't want my own kids to go through what I went through. I wanted them to have that love and that foundation until *they* were ready to leave.'

But it's also given her an ability to connect with young people who, for whatever reason, are feeling out of place.

'It's a commitment for me, and even when things are hard I won't give up easily. Because I want to do it. And when you see them settling down, making something of themselves, it's an achievement. In my life, there were maybe other achievements I would have liked, but certain things sort of prevented me from doing it. But this, knowing I'm doing a good job, I just want to keep on doing it.'

'Sometimes they'll have rice and peas with a piece of fish. They all like my fish and the way I cook it.'

Pan Fried Fish

Preparation Time: 25–30 minutes plus marinating
Cooking Time: 10 minutes
Serves: 4

INGREDIENTS
4 x approx 340g/12oz whole red snapper (headless, if you prefer), scaled and cleaned
2 tsp all purpose seasoning
1 tsp table salt
2 tsp freshly ground black pepper
3 small onions, peeled and sliced
1–2 (depending on how hot you like it!) scotch bonnet chillies, finely sliced
2 garlic cloves, peeled and finely chopped
4 tbsp white wine vinegar
1 red pepper, deseeded and sliced
1 green pepper, deseeded and sliced
1 yellow pepper, deseeded and sliced
Vegetable oil, for shallow frying

METHOD
1. Score the skin of the fish 2–3 times on each side.
2. In a large shallow dish, mix together the seasoning, salt and pepper. Rub the seasoning mixture all over the fish. Cover, chill and leave to marinate for at least half an hour or overnight, if possible.
3. In a large sauté pan, pour in enough oil to the depth of 2.5mm/ one-eighth". Heat the oil and fry the fish for 4–5 minutes on both sides (depending on the size of the fish) or until cooked through, crisp and golden. Remove with a slotted spatula and drain on a plate lined with kitchen paper.

4. Meanwhile, in a medium-sized frying pan, heat 3 tbsp of vegetable oil over a medium heat. Fry the onion for 2–3 minutes then add the chilli and garlic and fry for a further 2 minutes.
5. Stir in the vinegar and cook for 30 seconds.
6. Remove the pan from the heat and stir in the peppers.
7. Place the fish on a plate, scatter over the pepper mixture and serve with a portion of rice and peas.

Rice and Peas

Preparation Time: 15 minutes
Cooking Time: 20–25 minutes
Serves: 4

INGREDIENTS
1 x 420g tin kidney beans, rinsed and drained
1 onion, peeled and diced
30g/1oz coconut cream
2 tsp fresh thyme leaves or 1 tsp dried thyme
225g/8oz long grain rice, rinsed
30g/2oz unsalted butter
Salt and freshly ground black pepper

METHOD
1. Put the kidney beans, onion, coconut cream, thyme and 500ml/ 18fl oz water into a medium-sized saucepan. Season with salt and pepper and bring to the boil.
2. Stir in the rice and butter and bring back to the boil. Reduce the heat to a simmer, cover and cook for 20 minutes or until all the liquid has been absorbed.

Monica's Tip:
'Rice and peas are at the heart of Caribbean Cooking. We love to eat them with fish and curried mutton.'

FIONA our nutritionist says
All fish is good for you which is why nutritionists recommend that we should aim to eat fish at least twice a week. White fish like cod and red snapper are rich in protein and low in fat. Fish like salmon, mackerel and sardines are rich in omega-3 fats which will help to keep the heart and brain healthy.
Although rice and peas is not a vegetable, just 3 tablespoons of red kidney beans will count as one of the five portions of fruit and vegetables that we are all recommended to eat each day. Try to find beans canned without salt or sugar, or rinse well before using to remove salt.

Monica's Tip:
'If you're not comfortable preparing fish, ask your fishmonger for help.'

Sandie lives in the Croydon area and has been a foster carer with FCA for two years.
Her recipes are **Lemon Drizzle Cake and the "Sandie Special" Hot Chocolate**

Sandie

comfort

'We just felt we had something to offer. We had two spare bedrooms, a beautiful garden. And I just knew the boys would be supportive. So we decided to see what we could put back, what we had to offer.'

Getting involved

'I love what I do because although all of the children have their difficulties, and some of them can be very challenging, I find that there's always a chink in their armour. There's always some way that you can get to know them and find something that works for them.'

As a learning support assistant, Sandie had worked with looked after children in school, but it was meeting her eldest son's new girlfriend that made her seriously consider fostering.

'When Ashley first started going out with Laura she was in social services care. And so her social worker came down to see us, we had to get checked out and all that. I didn't know much about it until then, but seeing how much they were doing for her got me interested.'

Ashley and Laura eventually married, had twins and moved to live in the Midlands. Although Sandie's two younger sons were still living at home in Croydon, they were now independent. So she and her husband Gary talked it through.

'We felt that we had something to offer. We had two spare bedrooms, a beautiful garden, and, I knew, I just knew the boys would be supportive. So we decided to do something, to see what we could put back, what we had to offer.'

Sandie felt that what she'd learned by bringing up three boys would come in useful.

'Gary and me were always firm, a bit tough. Tough love, you know. Never over the top, but firm boundaries. And now, my sons say, blimey mum you were right. Because having children of their own they can understand.'

But going through the assessment process to become a foster carer helped her to realise that she could also draw upon her experiences in the classroom.

'I already knew that you have to find a way to reach them. In the early days when you meet a child you really have to get to know them. Their likes, their dislikes. What's important to that child.'

Facing the challenges

Sandie has now been a foster carer with FCA for two years, but even in this short time she has become aware that fostering is not always easy.

'We originally thought we'd foster older boys, but then we did think about girls as well. And once we were approved, our first call was about a girl, a sixteen-year-old girl. So we talked about it and decided, yes, we'd like to try to do it. So our first girl came to us on respite, two weekends a month to start with, and then three out of four weekends. Well, she was difficult – very, very challenging. And we did cope until she started absconding. Not only from her main carers, but then from us too. Which meant that I was always having to ring the police and the out-of-hours team to say that she'd gone missing. It was so bad that I got to know the out-of-hours team personally. It was like, it's Sandie again. She's not come home. OK, they'd say, we'll ring you later to see if there's any update – there never was. I came to realise that you can make your home as welcoming as possible, but if a child doesn't want to stay – for whatever reason – there's only so much you can do.'

There have been more positive experiences.

'We had one young woman with us for a week with severe ADHD. I'm not saying it wasn't hard work. She'd dance, and jump and leap around the kitchen. And she would talk the whole time. In fact, eating her dinner, she could hardly put a mouthful of food in her mouth because she was talking so much. But I work with children in school like that, and it didn't matter to me. This was just a child being joyful, if you like. It was a pleasure actually. You could see that she loved being with us. She lived with elderly grandparents, so I suppose she enjoyed being with a younger family.

'Hopefully a child will leave here saying, I enjoyed my stay with Sandie and Gary. I enjoyed playing the silly games we play as a whole family, the card games, helping me with my animals, or even me dragging them down to my greenhouse to do the gardening with me.'

'I didn't go into fostering with my eyes closed. You know that the children who come to you will have baggage. But you don't know until you open that suitcase what you are going to find.'

And she absolutely adored the cats – had one on her shoulder practically the whole time. So it was just pleasant, and really rewarding to have done that.'

However, it was Sandie's most recent placement which really put her commitment to fostering to the test.

'When our supervising social worker brought the paperwork to talk about it, and we read about the things she'd been involved in, even then we were thinking, oh, I don't know – could we do it? Would we really be able to do it? So I thought, well, the only way you're going to find out is to actually try.'

Even in the early days this young woman's behaviour was very challenging.

'When she arrived she had only been in school one month in the previous year. I have always believed that education is so important. It had been for my own boys, and I want the best for fostered children too. So Gary started taking her to school. But then her Oyster card arrived. And she actually said, can't I go to school by myself, can't you trust me? So we did. But we soon found out that she wasn't going at all. And she had been using her lunch money to go round London all day – not going to school at all.'

Finding things that work

Sandie does not give up easily, and thought very carefully about how she might reach this young woman.

'I had realised that her two favourite things were her mobile phone and going on the internet, talking to her friends. When she'd come to us she didn't have a mobile, but we'd given her one to use when she was out and about. So that we could contact her, make sure that she was safe, and she could keep in touch with us. And because her school is a long way away all her friends weren't local, so she loved the phone and she loved going on MSN – chatting with them all. So when I found out she wasn't going to school I said, OK, if there's no school, then there's no computer when you get home. And it worked! She actually started going to school every day which was fantastic.'

Sandie also understood that making this young woman feel comfortable in her new home was so important in building their relationship.

'When she first came she would only eat one particular food. I'd say, what d'you want to eat today? And she'd say, oh, anything. But if I put anything on her plate, she just wouldn't eat it. So I gave her a piece of paper and a pen and said, can you please write down the things you like to eat so I can go shopping and get exactly the foods you like. There it was, coco pops, toast, McDonalds, curry and sweet and sour chicken. And I've always been honest and direct with her, and I had to say, a lot of that is breakfast food and McDonalds is a treat, and not good to eat every day. So a lot of evenings it was just sweet and sour chicken. But that was OK. She was eating.'

Hot chocolate

Hot chocolate, especially the way that Sandie prepared and presented it, came to have a special meaning for them both.

'When she started going to school regularly I had to find a way to say thank you, to show I appreciated what she was doing. But I didn't want to use money as a reward. The life she'd been living – the messages about love and money were all mixed up. She didn't like tea or coffee, though she was partial to a cup of hot chocolate. So one evening I said, how d'you fancy a "Sandie Special"? What's that? Well, wait and see. And I was kind of chuckling to myself, and thinking, how am I going to make hot chocolate special? So I had some whipped cream in the fridge. Made a lovely cup of chocolate, squirted cream on top and then grated a bar of chocolate over. It looked beautiful, and she went, ohhhh, that looks good! Drank it, and she had this wonderful white moustache where she was licking her lips. And therein, the "Sandie Special" was born.'

In time, Sandie showed her how to make the drink for herself.

'She'd been watching me do it for a while. And the first time she tried we both laughed because it was such a mess. But every night she persevered, until one particular weekend. By then she had started going missing, and she had gone out with friends on the Friday after school and had not come back. I'd been up till all hours, worrying, hoping she'd come home safe. Then, on the Saturday I'd gone to bed at nine,

leaving Gary and the family downstairs, just too tired, exhausted. And she'd come in, and when she came back like that she'd often want the chocolate. The first thing she'd do, drink it, then have a bath. I wouldn't ask any questions, just give her her drink, run the bath – just wait for her to be ready to talk. But this time I was in bed, so she made it herself. I woke up, heard her squealing. Jumped up, thought, whatever's wrong? But she'd made the perfect "Sandie Special"! Just so pleased with herself and wanting to show me. She was so proud of herself. The delight on her face. And the nicest thing about it was that after that she started offering to make drinks for us. She'd never done that before.'

Sandie has always encouraged children and teenagers to cook with her.

'Normally, I try at least once to get them involved in making a cake. And the easiest one, the nicest one is my lemon drizzle cake. I get them to grate the lemons while we're going through the patter of the goodness of the lemons, how in this cake you're getting the goodness of the whole lemon. How the sharpness of the lemon contrasts with the sweetness from the sugar. By actually being involved in making it – because it's a simple recipe, not flashy – they can instantly see the success of something that they've been part of.'

'When it's warm and it comes out of the oven it's comforting, it's a pudding. But then once it cools down it's a cake. A fantastic cake that the family fight over.'

'When she came back she'd often want the chocolate. The first thing she'd do, drink it, then have a bath. I wouldn't ask any questions. Just give her her drink, run the bath – just wait for her to be ready to talk.'

In fact, lemon drizzle cake has become a favourite.

'When it's warm and it comes out of the oven they love it because it's comforting, it's a pudding. But then when it cools down it's a cake. Gary takes it to work, my grandchildren love it. I've even made it for my social worker, and she's taken it into the office because I wanted to thank the team for the help they've given me. In fact, I've even been asked to make it for meetings or for when us carers get together! It's just a fantastic cake that everyone fights over.'

Keeping going

Sadly, stories about fostering do not always have happy endings, and Sandie's most recent placement had to end when the young woman she was looking after could not be kept safe.

'She was staying away from us for longer periods, and the police became more involved. I built up a good relationship with them. We worked closely together and we tried really hard. Every time she came back it wasn't to get shouted at. I would tell her, people worry about you, people do care about you. But sometimes it's not enough. We couldn't break the vicious cycle of what she was doing. And we wanted her to learn to start liking herself, respecting herself, and I came to realise that we couldn't do that here. She needed to be in a place where she could get all the help she needed.'

It's been a difficult time for Sandie, but they continue to keep in touch, she has received good support and she is sure that she will keep on fostering.

'I didn't go into this with my eyes closed. You know that the children are going to have baggage. But you don't know until you open that suitcase what you're going to find.'

And her motivation remains clear.

'We became carers to be that special person for that child. For as long as can be, we'll be there – hopefully to see that child move on to better places. I just want them to leave here saying, I enjoyed being with Sandie and Gary. I enjoyed laughing with them. I enjoyed crying with them. I enjoyed playing the silly computer games that we play as a whole family. The card games, or cooking with them, or helping with the animals. Even me dragging them down to the greenhouse to help me with the gardening. And I'll try to help that child as much as I can, because that's what I want to do.'

Lemon Drizzle Cake

Preparation Time: 20–25 minutes
Cooking Time: 40–50 minutes
Serves: 12–16

INGREDIENTS

455g/1lb caster sugar, plus extra for dredging
455g/1lb margarine or unsalted butter, softened, plus extra for greasing
3 large eggs, lightly beaten
3 lemons, zest and juice
455g/1lb self-raising flour
Double cream, for serving

METHOD

1. Preheat the oven to 180C/350F/ Gas Mark 4. Lightly grease a 33cm/13" x 25.5cm/10" x 7.5cm/3" (or similar) baking tin then line with greaseproof paper or tinfoil.
2. In a medium-sized bowl or that of a food mixer, cream together the sugar and margarine, with electric beaters or a paddle, on a medium speed until light and fluffy.
3. Gradually beat in the eggs followed by the lemon zest.
4. Fold in the flour until combined.
5. Pour the mixture into the lined tin and bake for 40–50 minutes or until the cake is golden, springy to the touch and a skewer comes out clean.
6. Remove the cake from the oven, prick all over with a skewer then pour the lemon juice evenly over the cake and dredge with sugar.
7. If you can resist, allow the cake to cool; if not, serve immediately with cream for a comforting pudding.

"Sandie Special" (Hot Chocolate)

Preparation Time: 5 minutes
Cooking Time: 5 minutes
Makes: 1

INGREDIENTS

3 heaped tsp of your favourite instant hot chocolate drink
(that can be made with hot water)
Milk
Squirty cream

METHOD

1. Spoon the chocolate powder into your favourite heatproof cup.
2. Pour in enough boiled water until almost at the top. Stir well.
3. Top up with milk and finish with a good squirt of cream.

Sandie's Tip:
'Sometimes, I grate a small bar of chocolate on top of the hot chocolate as an extra special treat!'

FIONA our nutritionist says

Whatever their age, most children love cooking. Getting them to help you in the kitchen will teach them an important life skill and help them learn that cooking can be a fun and creative pastime. If you don't have a favourite recipe that you like to cook, why not get children to look through a cookery book or magazine and choose something that they would like to make.

FIONA our nutritionist says

Balance is a key ingredient in a healthy diet, which means as long as you balance the "not-so-good-for-you" foods with lots of "good-for-you" foods like fruit and vegetables then there is absolutely no reason why you can't enjoy the treats like hot chocolate. In fact, dairy products like milk, yoghurt and cheese are an excellent source of calcium which helps to keep bones healthy.

Sandie's Tip:
'I like to use the rough side of the grater for my lemon zest – just be careful not to catch too much of the bitter pith. If you would prefer a lighter cake to a pudding, beat more eggs into the mixture. This will take up to 7 large eggs.'

Stella is a local authority foster carer who grew up in Ghana, and now lives in Catford with Emmanuel and their adult son. Her recipe is **Chicken and Peanut Butter Soup with Rice Balls**

Stella

heritage

Growing up in Africa

Stella's home is in Catford where she lives with her husband Emmanuel and their adult son. But she grew up in Ghana, and she has very happy memories of that time.

'Well, my parents were both teachers and we lived in different towns and cities. My grandparents though, stayed in our village and I enjoyed being with them. I made sure that every holiday I spent there. Living the country life. Helping on the farm, helping with the plantation and everything. And that was really good for me because I had so many experiences. There were no books, you know, so in the evenings my grandparents would sit with me and tell me stories. Different stories. Which I did enjoy. And it made me a good storyteller too.'

She feels that her grandparents taught her so much, and helped her to become the woman she is today.

'We didn't have a lot of toys so we had to be creative. Make up our own games. We watched the grown-ups too. Copied what they did and tried to help. When my dad was at university and my mum doing her teacher training course, I was in the village for a long time and I remember every Sunday morning I would go to the market with my grandmother to sell things. We would dress up nicely, put enkanfu, that's yellow yam, in a basket. Carry it on our heads. Go round the village and then to market. I liked being with her, going with her. It felt good.'

She remembers very clearly the kinds of foods she loved to eat as a little girl.

'In the afternoon I loved bananas with peanuts. As a child, in the afternoon your grandparents would be working. So you would run home from school, change your clothes. Quickly wash your feet, cream your legs and face with cocoa butter. Then run to the farm where you would have your lunch. Nice fresh spinach, fresh palm oil, yams and fruit. Mangos, pears. Run back to school for the afternoon. But Sunday was best. That's when every family had a nice meal and when my grandmother would cook very nice. Chicken or goat, or sometimes soup. And that's when my grandfather would give us biscuits. Tiny, tiny, small round ones. For being good, for helping.'

Coming to London

Stella came to live in London in 1985, and for a time life became difficult.

'For the first ten years I did odd jobs. One cleaning job after another. Because I wasn't feeling good about myself. I went through a lot of bad patches, bad things. Lost my self-confidence, and I didn't think I could do things…There was no time to read, no time to look at the newspapers. Just lost my self-confidence. And then I met Emmanuel. He's from Ghana too. Ashanti, like me. And he said, oh Stella, you could be doing better things! You must go to college, study. I told him, no, no I can't! I cannot write, and I cannot remember my spellings. But he helped me, and he helped my confidence, and so I decided to go to college and train as a nursery nurse.'

After receiving her diploma, Stella began working in a school in South London.

'And I was so lucky to have a very dedicated and sympathetic head teacher. You know, she observed me, and she knew that I wasn't so confident and so she picked up on the one thing that I thought I could do well – that's my storytelling.'

With this woman's encouragement, Stella found a role for herself, showing other teachers and even parents how stories could be used to engage children and make learning fun. Stella took these skills to a new post in a local authority day centre, and it was there that her interest in foster care began.

'I was shocked because I had seen poverty in Africa. But I didn't expect that here. In the nursery I noticed that some children were coming to school without breakfast. Without loving care. And I decided, I think I would like to be a foster carer. You see, I'd grown up with many children at home. My mum, as a teacher, had brought many other children into our home and I had helped look after them. So I felt I had that skill and knowledge as well.'

'There were no books in the village, so my grandparents would sit with me and tell me stories. Which I did enjoy. And it made me a good storyteller too.'

'Now I am proud of who I am and my culture. And I want to pass that on to the children I look after.'

Looking after children

And so, in June 2000 and in her late forties, Stella approached her local authority and started fostering. Over the past nine years she has looked after a number of children, many of whom share her African heritage.

'They've been born in this country, and they know they are Ghanaian, or Nigerian. But for some that's all they know. When they come here me and Emmanuel will teach them, help them. Start with their names, talk about their country. Because I do know something about Nigeria. I lived there for a long time too. So we start with that. Then they hear me playing our music, talking our language, some phrases. They say, how do you know? And I'll talk about my experiences. On Saturday nights we'll put on the music and say, come and dance. And that's how I introduce them.'

Food has an important part to play in making these connections.

'I go to shops where we can buy African food. When we get there, some will recognise straight away. Oh, my auntie used to cook this. Or, my mum cooked this before. I'll say, shall we try? I'll buy, and we'll come home and cook. We all share, the adults and the children. We'll all cook and eat together.'

Sometimes the children and young people will introduce new food or particular dishes to Stella.

'One boy whose family is from the Caribbean asked, can we make dumplings because I've done that before? He showed me because he knows. We got the ingredients. We cooked dumplings. I had some. Emmanuel too. My daughter came to visit and asked to try. She said, mmm, not bad at all. It's really nice. Filling and nourishing. I'll cook it again. So I learn things too.'

Making a connection was especially important for one of the children Stella fostered.

'Her mum's dad is Ghanaian. When she came here and we saw her name, we talked about it. Because her name is from Gha, some of her people are Gha. But until then she didn't know. So we showed her pictures of Ghana and gave her a flag, and she took those things to school. Then last Christmas we got permission to take her to Ghana to visit our family. She met my grandmother who is now 101. And I took photos of her on the farm. Bought her our clothes. She was overwhelmed. She went from not understanding to feeling very proud of herself. It was hard work, but so good to see the change.'

This child also grew to like the African food Stella made for her.

'The fried plantain. She'd never tried that until she came here but now she loves it. And the rice balls we serve with the chicken soup, she always asks for them. Trying new things has not always been easy for her, but eating together, all together like we did in Africa, she does enjoy.'

Being an African woman

Preparing and sharing food continues to be an important part of Stella's life.

'At the weekend my daughter and her little girl come here. And with my other daughter we'll cook. Make the chicken and peanut soup with rice balls. Chop up some fresh fruit. Then we'll have a fun evening, like a picnic. If my son is around he'll join us, and the children too. I'll set up the table outside. Play African music and we dance. The girls living with us now, they love it.'

She believes that growing up in her village gave her the joy of sharing.

'I was brought up to respect. Not just adults – everyone. Children too. And to do things for others. Whatever you get, you don't keep it to yourself. You don't need it all. So you give some to others who don't have what you have.'

'Last Christmas we got permission to take her to Ghana to visit our family. It was so good to see the change in her.'

'At the weekend we'll cook.
Make the chicken and peanut butter soup with rice balls.'

This helps to explain why Stella is a foster carer, but her feelings as a young woman, new to London, have been an equally strong influence.

'When I first came here it was painful. When I started working I used to sit in the toilets in my lunch break to weep. Remembering the person I was back home. You see, back home I was a special person. A special person in my family. And when I came to London I became nothing. Some people would not look at you, would not talk to you. I am a sensitive person and it took me so long to get over it. So I can empathise with the children who come to me. How they might be feeling.'

Years later, with many achievements, Stella takes pride in being an African woman and her relationship with Ghana remains strong.

'There's a small group of about fifteen of us from my village in Ghana. And we meet once a month. Some of it is socialising, but we also give money. And we saved that money and used it to put in water and electricity in the village. Then, because we knew that the school back home had no books we thought about that. When I started working in schools and saw the damaged ones being thrown away, I started mending them. And they let me have the old books that they didn't use. Word got around that I was collecting books and parents gave me more. And so their library is full!'

Stella feels very happy when she visits her village and people recognise her.

'I say hello to everyone. They see me walking and come out of their homes. And I don't just walk by, I go in. The elders who knew my dad, they always say, you're just like your dad. You're carrying on what your dad did. Because now I am proud of who I am and of my culture. And I want to pass that on to my children and the children I look after. Make them feel good about who they are.'

Chicken and Peanut Butter Soup with Rice Balls

Preparation Time: 20–25 minutes
Cooking Time: 1 hour–1 hour and 5 minutes
Serves: 4–6

INGREDIENTS

For the soup
1 x 1.375kg/3lb chicken, cleaned and cut into 16 portions
4 small onions, peeled and chopped
1 tbsp ginger paste
1 heaped tsp garlic paste
600ml/21fl oz chicken stock
455g/1lb smooth peanut butter
1 x 400g tin plum tomatoes
1 red pepper, deseeded and roughly chopped
Salt, to taste

For the rice balls
70g/2½oz basmati rice, per person

METHOD

1. Place a large saucepan/casserole pot over a medium heat. Fry the chicken pieces, skin side down, for 10 minutes or until browned. Using tongs, turn the pieces of chicken over to seal the underside.
2. Stir in two of the onions, ginger and garlic for 5 minutes or until translucent and softened.
3. Pour in the chicken stock and season with salt. Bring to the boil then reduce the heat and simmer for 10 minutes.
4. In a small saucepan, mix together the peanut butter with 500ml/18fl oz water. Gently bring the mixture to the boil, stirring occasionally to prevent burning and a lumpy mixture. Gently simmer for 5–10 minutes or until the oil from the peanut butter settles on the surface.
5. In a food processor, blend together the remaining 2 onions with the tinned tomatoes and red pepper. Add this mixture to the chicken and simmer for 5 minutes.
6. Finally, add the peanut butter mixture to the chicken pan and simmer for a further 30 minutes.
7. Meanwhile, in a medium-sized saucepan, bring the rice to the boil in double its volume of water. Simmer for 10 minutes or until the rice is really soft and has absorbed all the water.
8. With a wooden spoon or hand blender, mash the rice until it sticks together. Divide the rice into four equal portions then, using a clean cloth to protect your hands, or 2 large serving spoons, mould each portion into a ball.
9. Serve the peanut butter soup with the rice balls.

Stella's Tip:
'In Ghana we do keep the skin and bones on the chicken to add flavour. But if you prefer, you can use skinless and boneless chicken instead with a really good chicken stock.'

FIONA our nutritionist says

A hearty bowl of soup is a great way to warm up on a chilly winter day and provides a filling and nutritious meal. All nuts are rich in protein and healthy fats but they are quite calorific, so if you're watching your weight use half the quantity of peanut butter.

Stella's Tip:
'I like to finish a meal with some really nice fresh fruit. Just chop it up, and let everyone help themselves.'

Justin and Dan are FCA carers who live in Frome. Their recipes are **Runner Bean Chutney** and **Raspberry Cordial**

Justin & Dan

resourceful

'It means a lot to me to
take on the parenting role
that I've always wanted.
We just love having him
here, and we miss him
when he's not here.

Thinking about fostering

'People do forget – they don't deliberately do it, it's not malicious – but they do forget that just because you're gay, you're still going to have maternal or paternal feelings. For me, I'd got to my late twenties, and before then it was the last thing on my mind to want kids. But then, at about thirty it suddenly kicked in, and I realised that I wanted children. And fulfilling that desire to be a parent is not the same for a gay man or woman. It's not just about meeting the right partner. It takes a lot of thinking about, a lot of thought.'

As a single gay man, Justin considered surrogacy and looked at the possibility of adoption.

'I went through all the options, and I did consider fostering too. But at that time, I was single and I didn't think I would be taken seriously. So it wasn't until about three years ago, and when an agency opened down the road from here, that I really did something about it.'

By this time, Justin was living with his partner Dan in Frome, a small town in the West Country.

'I'd had an interesting career, doing lots of different things, mostly related to catering. Dan works for the Health Service. He's more interested in the academic side of things. So we knew that I would be the full-time carer and that Dan would want to continue working, and maybe even go on to train as a doctor. And so when we heard that the agency was looking for new foster carers, we had thought it all through and decided to make an application.'

The couple began the assessment process, but things didn't go very well.

'I'm not going to say that they had a problem with us being gay, I'm not suggesting that. But they just didn't seem ready to work with us. They seemed to focus on the negative. All the discrimination we'd faced growing up. Had we been bullied at school, shouted at in the street? And neither of us had actually experienced that. They wanted us to draw upon experiences that we hadn't actually had, and it just felt false. We wanted to be treated as a couple being assessed for fostering, not as "the gay couple". And eventually we thought, if we're not comfortable now, we're never going to be comfortable as carers for

'The other evening I showed him how to use runner beans and carrots to make a vegetable quiche. Next time he'll be able to make it himself.'

them. So by mutual agreement we stopped.'

Then one of their friends brought round an advertisement from a local newspaper.

'It was FCA, and we had already heard about them, someone had already mentioned FCA to us. I was still wary, so it stayed in the kitchen for a couple of months, but then I did ring them and they visited. And this time it was so different. Right from the word go. They sent a social worker, but with a carer, who talked about what she'd been doing over the years, the children she'd looked after. But mainly it was just that throughout the assessment we were treated as individuals, it focused on what we'd done before, the strengths we might have to look after children, as well as the difficulties.'

Being parents

Justin and Dan were approved as foster carers for FCA, and their first placement was made in the summer of 2008.

'We were delighted to become foster carers. And then our first placement was a teenager. Both of our interests are very orientated towards the things that he is interested in. Sports, music, cars. Keeping fit. But before coming here he'd experienced a lot of neglect, really just been left to his own devices, missed a lot of school. Had run away from home, gone missing and no one had reported that for three weeks!'

Dan and Justin see helping this young man to catch up with things he's missed out on as an important part of their role, as Dan explains.

'He's lost so much time from school and when it really matters – his GCSE years. We're working very hard with social services now to get him into a college in this area when term starts again. But in the meantime, I know he's worried about his literacy and that he needs some help with that. My sister's a teacher, and she's offered us some materials and also some one-to-one time with him, just to build up his confidence again.'

In fact, the couple use every opportunity to encourage his desire to learn.

'A few weeks ago we took the dog for a walk up to a place called Cley Hill. It's Palaeolithic, and on top of the hill there's a Bronze Age burial mound. And he was so interested in that, and the idea that people might be buried there, but also their animals, their tools. We talked a lot about it. And I just thought he'd forget. Then, a couple of days later we were out there again, and he started talking about it all, he'd remembered every word. Soaked it all up like a sponge. It's the same with plants and nature. I'll ask him if he knows the names of different flowers, and tell him the Latin names too, and he really likes that.'

Doing it our way

They are also encouraging his interest in food and cooking.

'I think at home his dad always cooked, and that's probably the one thing they did do together. He really likes it. He had to do a work placement before he finished school for the summer, and we managed to sort something out through friends so that he went to a restaurant kitchen. He just lapped that up, did very well. Has a flair for it and wants to learn more about kitchen skills and techniques.'

Both men share this enthusiasm too, but at home it is usually Justin who makes most of their meals.

'Dan's mum was married to an Italian and he grew up eating Mediterranean food because she's a chef and that's what she prepared for the family. But his working hours mean that it's more likely that I'll cook. Especially because he makes such a colossal mess whenever he's in the kitchen!'

The couple have an allotment where they are able to grow their own fruit and vegetables.

'We both like to use seasonal produce. We make jam, and we make chutney. We don't like waste and so we'll use, say, a glut of tomatoes, to make our own pasta sauce from scratch which we'll freeze. Or when we've got plenty of raspberries we'll adapt Dan's elderflower cordial which his mum always does, and use raspberries instead. It makes a lovely refreshing drink that's a bit different. And you can freeze it to make granita – a great Italian pudding for the summer.'

Their foster son is also a keen gardener who helps out on the allotment, and is therefore able to see at first hand how what they grow can be used to make healthy but inexpensive food.

'The other evening I said, I'm going to use these carrots and these runner beans in a vegetable quiche. He asked if he could watch, and I showed him how to make pastry. Next time he'll be able to do it himself. And these are skills that will stay with him.'

They are not only promoting his independence, but, as Dan suggests, it is also helping him to think about the future.

'He's become very focused on what he wants, and he's clear that he wants to be a chef. And with that attitude I know he will do it, he will get where he wants to be. That's such a shift because he had been very easily led, and before he came here he had been getting into all kinds of trouble.'

'When I was his age I wasn't having a very nice time. So it's actually just so rewarding to make someone smile and feel good about themself.'

'We adapt Dan's elderflower cordial and we use raspberries instead. It makes a lovely refreshing drink.'

Making a difference

Dan feels very pleased that their agency and social services believed that this was the right placement, even though they are new carers.

'His social worker is so good, and has spent the time to get to know him, and does really think about his needs. So they went out of their way to find foster carers who shared his interests and where he could settle and feel cared for. And they are very happy with the way things are going because we've got lots of plans. He's got so much energy and loves the outdoors, and I have a good friend at work who's a real action woman who wants to start him diving, in the pool to start with, and maybe even potholing. He's excited about trying it all.'

And they are both delighted that he is happy in their home.

'We've been so lucky with him. He's the first young person to come here, and we were ready to expect all kinds of problems. But he's kind, he's thoughtful and polite – incredibly polite. We've got a gem.'

Justin feels that fostering is giving him the opportunity to be a parent.

'It means a lot to me to take on the parenting role that I've always wanted. I think that many gay people are like

us and have, you know, abilities and skills which could be used to look after a young person, be it a boy or girl. All I know is that I love having him here and I miss him when he's not around. And the other day when he'd gone for contact, I went up to his room to get his washing and it was such a mess. And I said to Dan, you know, I always wanted a room that was a real mess because then you know there's a teenager living in it!'

Dan is motivated by his own experience.

'When I was his age I wasn't having a very nice time at all because my mum has a drink problem and I had quite a difficult background. So it's actually just so nice to make someone smile and make someone feel good. That's what I get out of it.'

And he welcomes the chance they have to make a difference.

'It's really rewarding. You can have an impact on someone's life. It may not be instantaneous, it may not happen straight away. But you may have given them some encouragement, helped to push them in a direction. Whether it's going to college, getting a job, just something simple. Something that shows them how stability feels. And what it means to feel good about yourself, to have self-respect.'

'We both like seasonal produce.
We make jam, and we make chutney.'

Runner Bean Chutney

Preparation Time: 20–25 minutes
Cooking Time: 45–55 minutes, plus cooling
Makes: 4 x 500ml preserving jars

INGREDIENTS

1kg/2lb 3oz runner beans, washed, topped, tailed and chopped
800g/1lb 12oz onions, peeled and chopped
850ml/1½pts malt vinegar
30g/1oz cornflour
1 heaped tbsp mustard powder
1 level tbsp turmeric
225g/8oz soft light brown sugar
455g/1lb demerara sugar

METHOD

1. In a large saucepan, boil the beans for 5 minutes then drain well.
2. In a separate large saucepan, simmer the onions with 250ml/9fl oz of the vinegar for 15–20 minutes or until softened and all the liquid has evaporated.
3. In a small bowl, mix together the cornflour, mustard powder and turmeric. Add 3 tbsp of the vinegar to form a paste.
4. Add the beans and the remaining vinegar to the onions and boil for 10 minutes.
5. Stir in the sugars until dissolved, followed by the cornflour mixture and simmer for a further 15–20 minutes or until thickened.
6. Sterilise the jars by filling them with boiling water and emptying them. Divide the mixture between the warmed sterilised jars. Leave to cool before sealing and chilling.

Justin's Tip:
'This chutney is best served simply. Have it with a very good strong cheddar cheese and some crackers, or try it in a ham sandwich'.

Raspberry Cordial

Preparation Time: 5 minutes
Cooking Time: 12–15 minutes, plus cooling
Makes: approximately 1 litre

INGREDIENTS

570g/1lb 4oz fresh raspberries, rinsed
285g/10oz caster sugar
Juice of 1 lemon
450ml/15fl oz water

METHOD

1. In a large saucepan, bring the sugar, lemon juice and water to the boil, stirring until the sugar has dissolved.
2. Stir in the raspberries and simmer for 8–10 minutes until the raspberries have softened. Remove the pan from the heat and leave to cool for 5 minutes.
3. Sieve the raspberry mixture over a jug, discarding the pulp.
4. Allow the cordial to cool, bottle and chill.

Dan's Tip:
'We found this cordial not only makes a refreshing drink but it can also be easily turned into a delicious raspberry granita. If you grow your own raspberries they certainly will not go to waste.'

FIONA our nutritionist says

If you're lucky enough to live near a pick-your-own farm, why not organise a family day out to pick some runner beans. Or if you have a large enough garden you could even try growing beans and some other vegetables at home. A visit to a pick-your-own farm is a fun day out and children are often more interested in eating fruit and vegetables that they have picked themselves.

FIONA our nutritionist says

Children can easily become dehydrated, particularly if they are very active, so it's important to encourage them to drink regularly. Water is the healthiest thing to drink but sometimes they want something a little more exciting. Dilute this cordial well to avoid giving children too much sugar or, when the weather is hot, use it to make ice lollies or home-made jelly.

Andi lives in a small market town in the West Country. After 23 years in fostering, she now helps to recruit and train new carers.
Her recipe is **Hippy Cake**

Andi

home

'This house has a history now....
overall it's been a happy house.
Because it has meant so much,
and to so many people.'

A life-changing moment

'I think things happen for a reason, I don't believe in coincidences. And so I was in the local library one day, and this bookmark fell out of a book. It was advertising a new scheme called Teencare, for fostering teenagers. I had thought about fostering before, just simply because I love children, I've always loved babies and children. And when I had thought about fostering, I'd dismissed it as fast, because my George was still young and I didn't want him to feel pushed out, I knew that wouldn't work. But I didn't know that anyone needed you to foster teenagers. So that leaflet got me thinking, it started something. That was twenty-three years ago, and it changed my life!'

As a lone mother with sons of thirteen, nine and George under two, Andi was finding it very hard to cope financially and feared that they might lose the home they loved.

'I'd struggled on for as long as I could, but because George was so badly affected by the break-up and quite clingy to me, I thought, well, if I do go back to work everything I've been doing to build up his confidence again will be lost, we'll be back to square one. So I needed to be able to work from home. And the Teencare scheme was offering what they called a fee element. So honestly, at the time that was part of the appeal, and I decided to find out more.'

Andi went to a meeting for prospective carers. But what she heard there made her think again.

'They wanted people who could look after teenagers with challenging behaviour, and I remember that they talked about smearing. And I had never come across that before, and I thought ah, no, this isn't for me, I can't do this. And so I rang the number I'd been given to ring the next day, and said, no, I've changed my mind. To this day I don't know how, and I don't remember his name – just that he was a social worker in Weston Super Mare – this guy must have seen something in me, something about me worth pursuing, because he asked me to think again, came round to talk to me about it. Spent time to explain, but without being pushy. And so I did do the training, and I think about six months from beginning to end, I had my first young person come and live here.'

I never give up

Over the following years many young people came to the house in Keynsham, near Bristol, where Andi still lives today.

'From the start I always had teenagers, and often multiple placements. Because it's a big house, and I had two spare bedrooms. At this stage I was fostering for the local authority and they were always needing me to take a second, and then a third placement. But they always had their own rooms because I just built on, just built on. Once there were identical twins who couldn't live with each other, and couldn't live without each other. And once a young girl who came to stay just for one night, in an emergency, and so I put her in with the other girls in this big bedroom. Then, after that first night she cried, and didn't want to leave. I didn't know at the time that she was pregnant. So I thought, well, the only way that she could stay would be to have that room divided. So I got a builder to come and he divided the room into two, so that made two rooms. Later, I had a loft extension done. Because all young people need their own space. That's so important.'

Despite her early misgivings, Andi found that this role suited her.

'Fostering is certainly something that you learn as you go along. You could do all the training in the world, but nobody can really prepare you for that first young person walking through your door. I'm not saying that training and preparation aren't very important because they are. But I am very, very aware that no matter what you're told about what can happen, until that young person walks in you can't really get your head around what it's going to be like. And I think the reason that I coped was because there was something clear in my mind. Anyone who came here, I wouldn't

'You can't just give up on them. And for the ones that do need me, I will always be here.'

'I've built my home around them. Not made silly rules that I know will be broken, and tried to accept them for who they are.'

give up on. Because I was aware that with every breakdown in placement they must surely be hurt more. And most have been hurt enough already. Even right from the beginning, it was such a strong feeling that I couldn't give up on them. And then I discovered that I have this capacity not to give up. I soon found out what I might have to cope with, and later I actually expected it. And so I was ready to deal with the bad times when they came. But it was something that I found that I could do, and do well. And something that I came to enjoy.'

Andi became very skilled at looking after teenagers with the most complex needs.

'Over the years I guess I gained a reputation for being able to take the teenagers whom no one else could manage. I've had young people here who could be very, very difficult to live with at times. The support has always been there for me, and I have needed it. But I think I've hung on in there because I adapted my life around them. So rather than chuck them out for behaviour that most people couldn't tolerate, I've built my home around them. Not made silly rules that I know will be broken, but tried to accept them for who they are. Because for some, I couldn't completely change their lives. Too much had already happened. But they did need a home and a safe place to live at that time, and for many I have been able to provide it.'

Being there

The ability to help these young people feel at home included recognising that they have families of their own.

'I sometimes think that we don't give enough thought to birth families. If I had to watch somebody else bring up my child, who for whatever reason I was unable to bring up myself, I think it would be the end for me. And to have to go into that person's house, which may well be a more luxurious home, to see that person doing all the things I should be doing with my child…it would just be too much. So I've always tried to make any of the meetings held here as comfy as possible for everyone, and that includes providing food.'

One particular cake Andi baked over the years has

'You can use the same mixture and put it in bun cases and the little ones love helping to do that.'

particular meaning for her fostered teenagers.

'Probably my fostering career didn't allow me to be the cook that's really inside me. Because honestly, they didn't want to eat the healthy stuff that I would have chosen to make. But there was one cake that I always liked to produce when we had a review here. Those meetings could be the most fraught because of course their parents would often come. And I wanted everyone to feel welcome, to feel at ease. I preferred to make my own fruit cake then, rather than just open a packet of shop-bought biscuits. It came out so often that it came to be known as review cake. But my first lot of teenagers always called it Hippy Cake. Because it was homemade, and I used organic ingredients before it was really fashionable to do that. They didn't really like it – people would be saying, oh, this cake's lovely and they'd be saying, where's the chocolate biscuits?! I became famous for that cake. And the kids do all remember it, laugh about it – even now when they get together.'

As these shared memories suggest, strong and lasting relationships were made under Andi's roof, especially between the young people.

'They can last a lifetime. Especially with the internet. They're always ringing me and telling me, I've been talking to so-and-so, and filling me in on what's going on. And some have really been there for each other. One of the girls who was here never really got it together. She had a serious drink problem, and she died when she was only in her twenties. It was tragic. But in her last days it was the other girls who had been here at the same time who rallied round. Do you know, when she died in the hospital it was those girls who went in to bath and dress her. And I asked them, why did you do that? And they said, because she was our sister, Andi. Why wouldn't we do that for our sister?'

They might also share more happy moments.

'Often when they come here what they usually want is to get the photos out. So I'll go and get the boxes of photos. They'll show each other – look at me here, do you remember this or that? And we'll end up laughing

'My first lot of teenagers called it Hippy Cake. Because it was homemade, and I used organic ingredients before it was really fashionable to do that.'

until the tears are streaming down our faces. Because even the times that were scary, the times that might have made me give up or wonder why I was doing this, when you look back on them together and you're feeling safe, you can laugh and laugh and laugh.'

The caring goes on

The bonds made with Andi and her sons also continue long after leaving her home.

'Even if I don't always see them I'll get phone calls. It might be when they're in trouble, or it might be good news or just to catch up. You see the difficult part about fostering can be that there's a cut-off point when they leave care. But you wouldn't turn out your own kids, would you? So how are these kids supposed to manage? They can't. They just can't. And you can't just give up on them. OK, some are doing alright and they won't need me and that's fine. But others haven't got anyone else. And for the ones that do need me, I will always be here.'

Many visit the house in Keynsham, bringing their own children.

'Yes, I'm meeting their sons and daughters now and they're eating my Hippy Cake! You can use the same mixture and put it in bun cases and the little ones love helping to do that. So we're passing those traditions along with all of the memories on to the next generation.'

Andi's youngest son, George, grew up in a fostering household.

'Through George especially, the bond goes on. Because he now lives in London, and if I get a call about someone in trouble down there, I'll call George. And at times he has gone from one side of London to the other, with a packet of cigarettes for someone who's been arrested, or to take some money, whatever it is. He's under no obligation to do that. But they were part of his childhood, you see. That's just very, very special.'

And she is now using all of her experience to recruit and train new foster carers.

'I go out and meet people interested in fostering, and I help to run the Skills to Foster course and I love doing that. Because I can tell it like it is, can't I?

It's one thing hearing about it from a social worker. But it's a different thing altogether from someone who's actually done it.'

No regrets

Andi is very clear that the more than twenty years she has spent as a foster carer have not always been easy for her, or her family.

'But it's been so much our life. We are known in our community for what we've done here. And I couldn't have done it without the help I've received – including from our local police station. In fact, I still roast the potatoes for the Keynsham police station Christmas lunch because I've always had the double oven to cook for all of my kids. And the Inspector up there once told me, do you know that 90 per cent of all the crime in this town came from your address?! We did laugh.'

She feels that she has learned a great deal.

'I've no regrets whatsoever. Alright, it was difficult. But I truly, truly believe that all of the kids who came to me were meant to be part of my life. And it sounds a bit twee when I'm saying it, but they have enriched my life. I've just had an amazing life with them, and I wouldn't have had it any other way.'

It helped to shape the men her sons have become.

'They've just been amazing. People used to say to me, aren't you worried about the effect that fostering must have on your children? But coming out of the other side now, I can look back and say, I'm so proud of my boys. They've grown up to be really sympathetic, understanding adults and I do think that – although they might say it's despite mum fostering – I know it's *because* mum fostered.'

And that it has given her home in Keynsham a special quality.

'This house has got a history now. It has lent itself to me to do the work that I've done in it. It's been battered, battered in lots of places by children who've had so much anger because of what's been done to them. But overall it's been a very happy house. In fact, the other day George came home and said, mum, if you ever move, before you do, we've got to have a big party. We've got to get everyone back here in this house. Because it has meant so much, and to so many people.'

Hippy Cake

Preparation Time: 10 minutes
Cooking Time: 1 hour and 20–25 minutes, plus cooling
Serves: 12

INGREDIENTS

For the cake
225g/8oz organic unrefined sugar
170g/6oz organic sultanas
115g/4oz organic butter
225ml/8fl oz organic whole milk
225g/8oz organic wholemeal
self-raising flour
1 level tsp baking powder
1 level tsp mixed spice
2 large organic eggs, beaten
Oil and flour, for preparing the cake
tin

For the icing
110g/4oz natural golden icing sugar,
sieved
1 tbsp water

FIONA our nutritionist says

Using wholemeal flour to make cakes and biscuits will boost the dietary fibre in the recipe. Fibre helps to keep the digestive system healthy. Other foods rich in fibre include wholemeal bread, wholegrain breakfast cereals, fruit and vegetables and beans and pulses.

METHOD

1. Preheat the oven to 150C/300F/Gas Mark 2. Grease a non-stick loose bottomed 17.5cm/7" diameter, 7.5cm/3" deep cake tin with a little oil. Dust with flour and shake out any excess.

2. Put the sugar, sultanas, butter and milk into a large saucepan and bring to the boil. Reduce the heat and simmer for 5 minutes. Remove from the heat and leave to cool for 10 minutes.

3. In a medium-sized bowl, mix together the flour, baking powder and mixed spice.

4. Fold the flour into the cooled milk mixture followed by the eggs.

5. Pour the cake mixture into the prepared tin and bake for 1 hour 15 minutes, or until evenly browned and when a skewer comes out clean. ('I use a knitting needle!')

6. Allow the cake to cool a little before turning it out onto a wire rack.

7. Once the cake has cooled, make the icing. In a bowl, mix together the icing sugar and water. When you have a smooth mixture, drizzle liberally over the top of the cake.

Andi's Tip:

'The cake mixture can also be used to make individual cakes. Line a 12-hole bun tin with paper cases. Evenly divide the cake mixture between the paper cases and place in a preheated oven at 200C/400F/Gas Mark 6 for 20–25 minutes. Once cooled, drizzle with icing. I found my children love to eat these, as well as make them.'

Abid and Shabnam live in Birmingham, and have been FCA carers for ten years. Their recipes are **Mixed Indian Vegetarian Dishes**

Abid & Shabnam

faith

'Here we were in this family house, just the two of us. And we knew there was a shortage of foster carers for Muslim children.'

Opening up our home

'Our two sons had grown up. They'd both gone to London, to university, to study. And here we were in this family house, just the two of us. Then, Shabnam read an article in the paper saying that there was a shortage of foster carers for Muslim children. Children whose needs could not be fully met because there aren't enough carers from the same background. We are both Indian Muslims, and so that was another important reason for taking the step.'

'Yes, and I've always loved children. We thought here we are, our own children are all grown up, there are other children, and we have the space and the time for them. Maybe it is something we could do.'

Abid and Shabnam did take the next step, and applied to become foster carers. They have now been with FCA for ten years.

'We'd had no experience of fostering whatsoever before, and we didn't know anybody who'd been doing it. But we had shared a home with my brother's family at one time, and we had lived with five children in the house. And my sister-in-law went out to work, so Shabnam had been caring for them all. That experience turned out to be very useful when we had our first placement.'

After approval, the first children who came to live with the couple were a group of four siblings.

'There were two boys and two girls, brothers and sisters. The youngest was four, and the eldest boy was twelve. They were dual heritage, white and Bangladeshi, and although they didn't speak the language, they had been brought up to understand some things about their culture.'

Shabnam is very honest about the impact of their arrival.

'It was chaotic to start with! Very difficult in the beginning. Because the children had been through some troubled times. And there was a lot of learning for us to do.'

Abid was aware that it was the eldest boy who found it hardest to settle.

'He had been like a father to the younger ones for a long time and so he didn't communicate well with us to start with. He was very guarded. So I took it slowly with him. He began to see for himself that we cared about them, and wanted to take good care of them all. And I started to bring him here into our sitting room every couple of weeks for our own time. A man-to-man talk. Sit him down. Talk to him and make him feel more relaxed and easy. So slowly, slowly it began to get better.'

Feeding a large family

They were both concerned about making the children welcome.

'It was a learning process for us, because we wanted to get to know them as individuals, their habits and ways. And not to impose any rules that they hadn't been used to. That would make them feel uncomfortable here.'

Shabnam, who loves to cook, was particularly anxious about making sure that they all ate well.

'At the beginning, I would ask each child, what would you like for dinner today? Someone would say, chicken curry. Another wanted kebab or some other meat. The youngest, just some rice. Even rice with chips! And then I was cooking sometimes five different meals. I would be in the kitchen for hours!'

'Yes, Shabnam was tired all the time. She was exhausted by it, and falling asleep in front of the TV. We talked, and decided that we had to find a different way.'

The couple came up with a very creative solution.

'I'd said to Shabnam, you can't go on cooking for individuals like this. And we'd noticed that each child would actually eat everything. It wasn't that one didn't

'Give them time, and give them love.'

'At home we like all kinds of food, but I love cooking Indian dishes from our own region.'

like chips – it's just that if you asked, they might not fancy chips that day! So she said, look, I'm going to give each child one day when it's their choice of meal. But we'll all eat what they choose that day. We sat down with the children together and Shabnam explained. Today is your turn, tomorrow's yours, next day for you and so on. To be honest, they weren't sure to start with. They'd become used to the individual meals every day! But they did agree to try.'

'Yes, it worked because they saw that on their day we ate the same food too. We also ate what they had chosen. But of course with all of us – the four children, myself, Abid – there was still one day left. The seventh day was Sunday. So we decided that on Sundays we'd have take-away! I'd get a rest from cooking and the children would have a treat. So that's how we did it!'

Over time, all of the children became more adventurous and keen to try the regional Indian food that Shabnam prepares so well.

'As a family we always ate all kinds of food. Chinese, English, fish and chips. But I do love to cook Asian food and they all liked to try what I make, especially the little snacks. Things like aubergine, lentil burgers, different vegetables. Those kind of dishes are very good for children when they come in from school feeling hungry. They are snacks. But they're healthy snacks. And very tasty.'

'One of the girls still asks for my recipes. Because each house is different. People may prepare the same food, but we all add our own touches.'

Shabnam's Tip:

'These dishes are best served with parathas or other Indian breads.'

Putting the foundations in place

All of these children lived with Abid and Shabnam until they left care, and the youngest girl is still with them.

'She was four when she came and she's fifteen now. She's doing very well at school and has ambitions to work with children with disabilities. We've tried to encourage that, and tried to give her the stability that her brothers and sisters didn't always have once they left our home.'

Even though they sometimes didn't take Abid's advice at the time, he has remained a strong influence.

'The eldest is now twenty-two and he's gone through a lot of changes in his life. Yet, every now and then he will phone me and tell me what he's doing. Then he'll ask, uncle, what do you think I should do?'

And they all remember Shabnam's cooking.

'One of the girls comes to see me regularly and she asks for my recipes, wants me to show her how to make the dishes she really liked. Because each house is different. People may prepare the same food, but we all add our own touches. And she wants to eat what she ate here.'

Abid shares their recipe for success in fostering.

'Communication is the key, just as it is with bringing up your own children And keep on trying. Take them in as part of your family, and most children will come around and settle. Because children do understand. Given time, they will recognise that you mean well and that you want the best for them. That you believe in them.'

Shabnam agrees.

'Yes. Give them time, and give them love.'

FIONA our nutritionist says

Most children are ravenous when they arrive home from school. They need regular snacks, but it's important not to let them fill up with sweets or biscuits, and then not want to eat their meal. This is a good time to introduce them to more interesting foods and flavours like Shabnam's spicy dishes.

Mixed Indian Vegetarian Dishes

Spiced Okra with Cashew Nuts

Preparation Time: 20 minutes
Cooking Time: 12–15 minutes
Serves: 4–6 as a side dish

INGREDIENTS
225g/8oz okra, washed and dried thoroughly
3 tbsp vegetable oil
1 small onion, peeled and sliced
60g/2oz cashew nuts
3–4 garlic cloves, peeled and crushed
3.7cm/1½" piece fresh root ginger, peeled and finely grated
1 large green chilli, deseeded and finely chopped or ¼ tsp red chilli powder
1 level tsp cumin seeds
Salt, to taste
Paratha, naan or chapatti, to serve

METHOD
1. Cut okra into quarters.
2. Heat the oil in a medium-sized frying pan over a medium heat.
3. Fry the onions for 4 minutes or until lightly browned.
4. Meanwhile, in a small frying pan, toast the cashew nuts over a low to medium heat until golden.
5. Add the garlic, ginger, chilli and cumin seeds to the onion and fry for a further minute.
6. Stir in the okra until well coated, and stir-fry for 4–5 minutes. Add a drop of water if the spices start to stick to the base of the pan.
7. Add the cashew nuts and cook until warmed through.
8. Season with salt and serve with paratha, naan or chapati.

Spinach and Paneer

Preparation Time: 15 minutes
Cooking Time: 12–15 minutes
Serves: 4–6 as a side dish

INGREDIENTS

2 tbsp vegetable oil
1 small onion, peeled and sliced
2–3 garlic cloves, peeled and crushed
1 heaped tsp ground cumin
½ heaped tsp chilli powder
½ heaped tsp turmeric
1 tbsp lemon juice
225g/8oz spinach, washed, drained and chopped
2 x 227g packet of paneer, cubed
2 tbsp mayonnaise
Salt, to taste
Salad, to serve

METHOD

1. Heat the oil in a large frying pan over a medium heat. Fry the onions for 3–4 minutes or until lightly browned.
2. Add the garlic, cumin, chilli and turmeric and fry for a further minute.
3. Mix in the lemon juice and spinach until just wilted.
4. Stir in the paneer for 3 minutes or until warmed through.
5. Fold in the mayonnaise.
6. Serve.

Stir-fried Aubergine

Preparation Time: 5–10 minutes
Cooking Time: 5–10 minutes
Serves: 4–6 as a side dish

INGREDIENTS

3 tbsp groundnut oil
1 aubergine, chopped
2–3 spring onions, trimmed and sliced diagonally
1 garlic clove, peeled and crushed
1 red pepper, deseeded and chopped
2 tbsp oyster sauce

1 tbsp tinned black beans
½ tsp ground black pepper
1 tbsp chopped fresh coriander

METHOD

1. Heat 2 tbsp of the oil in a wok or large frying pan. Stir-fry the aubergine for 2 minutes.
2. Add the remaining oil, onion, garlic and pepper and fry for a further 2 minutes.
3. Stir in the oyster sauce, beans and black pepper and cook for 1 minute.
4. Serve garnished with coriander.

Lentil Burgers

Preparation Time: 20 minutes, plus cooling and chilling
Cooking Time: 20 minutes
Serves: 4–6

INGREDIENTS

115g/4oz red or green lentils
115g/4oz mushrooms, wiped and finely chopped
115g/4oz courgette, finely chopped
60g/2oz cauliflower, finely chopped
275ml/10fl oz vegetable stock
2 tbsp chopped fresh flat leaf parsley
2 tsp chopped dill
85g/3oz oat flakes
Vegetable oil, for frying
Freshly ground black pepper

METHOD

1. Place all the ingredients except the oat flakes, oil and pepper into a large saucepan and bring to the boil. Cover and cook over a medium heat for 10 minutes or until the lentils are cooked.
2. Drain the lentils and vegetables and leave to cool for approximately 30 minutes. Season with pepper.
3. Mash the cooled lentils and vegetables. Divide the mash into 4–6 equal portions and shape each portion into a burger.
4. Tip the oat flakes into a dish and coat each burger with an even layer. If you have time, chill the burgers for 1 hour.
5. Cover the base of a medium-sized frying pan with a thin layer of oil and place over a medium heat. Fry the burgers for 2–2½ minutes on each side or until heated through and golden.
6. Serve.

Yam Curry

Preparation Time: 10 minutes
Cooking Time: 30–35 minutes
Serves: 2 or 4 as a side dish

INGREDIENTS

455g/1lb yam or sweet potato, peeled and cubed
2 tbsp vegetable oil
2 small onions, peeled and chopped
1 heaped tsp cumin seeds
1 heaped tbsp ground coriander
1 tsp ground turmeric
¼ tsp garam masala, plus extra for garnish
¼ tsp chilli powder, or more if you prefer
2 heaped tsp garlic paste
2 heaped tsp ginger paste
400ml/14fl oz low fat natural yoghurt
500ml/17fl oz water
2 heaped tbsp chopped fresh coriander
Salt, to taste
Vegetable oil, for deep frying

METHOD

1. Third-fill a medium saucepan with vegetable oil and place over a medium heat. To test if the oil is at the correct temperature for deep frying, drop in a small cube of bread. If it rises to the top and crisps up, the oil is ready.
2. Deep fry the yam in two batches. When the yam rises to the top, becomes slightly crisp and golden, remove with a slotted spoon and place in a bowl of boiled water, to remove excess oil. Be careful not to get the spoon wet during this process as it will spit when you return it to the pan of oil. Transfer the yam to a plate lined with kitchen paper, to drain.
3. Heat 2 tbsp of oil in a large frying pan over a medium–high heat. Fry the onion for 4–5 minutes until golden brown.
4. Add the cumin seeds, coriander, turmeric, garam masala, chilli, garlic and ginger and fry for 2 minutes.
5. Stir in the yoghurt and cook over a medium heat for 8 minutes or until a paste is formed. The mixture will pull away from the pan when it is ready.
6. Pour in the water and bring to the boil.
7. Add the yam and simmer for 6–8 minutes or until thickened to your liking.
8. Serve with a sprinkling of coriander and garam masala.

Thank you

Jackie, Alan, Vernon, Jennifer, Dee, Sally, Monica, Sandie, Stella, Emmanuel, Justin, Dan, Andi, Abid, Shabnam and their families and friends. To Margaret and Chris for their support. To those who read and encouraged. And, above all, to Jan who believed in this project.

Do YOU have the qualities to be a foster carer?

home
respect
family
comfort
heritage
history
acceptance
faith
memories
resourceful

Would you like to know more about fostering?

If reading this book has made you interested in foster carers and what they do you can find out more by visiting the BAAF website:
www.baaf.org.uk

There you will find links to useful resources, including:
First Questions on Fostering
Publications on Fostering

There is information about additional resources on BAAF's Be My Parent website:
www.bemyparent.org.uk

The Fostering Network also has answers to frequently asked questions and suggested reading on their website:
www.fostering.net

Are you interested in becoming a foster carer?

We need more foster carers and if you feel that this is something you could do, you should contact a fostering agency in your area. This could be a local authority agency, a voluntary agency or an independent fostering provider (IFP).

You can find a list of agencies in your area by using the Find an Agency database on the BAAF website:
www.baaf.org.uk

The Fostering Network's website has advice on choosing an agency:
www.fostering.net

Foster Care Associates (FCA) is the UK's leading independent fostering provider. They have local offices and so if you are interested in finding out more about becoming a foster carer for FCA, you can call your local foster carer recruitment team on **freephone: 0800 085 2225**

Or log on to the FCA website:
www.iwanttofoster.com